How Fashion Works

Couture, Ready-to-Wear and Mass Production

Gavin Waddell

Blackwell
Science

© 2004 by Blackwell Science Ltd,
a Blackwell Publishing Company

Editorial offices:
Blackwell Science Ltd, 9600 Garsington Road, Oxford OX4 2DQ, UK
 Tel: +44 (0)1865 776868
Blackwell Publishing Professional, 2121 State Avenue, Ames, Iowa 50014-8300, USA
 Tel: +1 515 292 0140
Blackwell Science Asia Pty Ltd, 550 Swanston Street, Carlton, Victoria 3053, Australia
 Tel: +61 (0)3 8359 1011

First published 2004

Library of Congress Cataloging-in-Publication Data
Waddell, Gavin.
  How fashion works: couture, ready-to-wear, and mass production/Gavin Waddell.
    p. cm.
  Includes bibliographical references and index.
  ISBN 0-632-05752-1 (pbk.: alk. paper)
  1. Clothing trade. 2. Fashion. I. Title.

TT497.W33 2004
391–dc22
2004001481

ISBN 0-632-05752-1

A catalogue record for this title is available from the British Library

Set in 10/12.5pt Sabon
by Marie Doherty, Havant, Hants
Printed and bound in India
by Replika Press Pvt Ltd, Kundli

For further information on Blackwell Publishing, visit our website:
www.blackwellpublishing.com

Acknowledgements

The author would like to thank those individuals, organisations and companies whose kindness and generosity have made this book possible.

Winifred Aldrich
Archivio G.B. Giorgini
Paola Arosio of Camera
  Nazionale della Moda
  Italiana
assyst bullmer
Sylvia Ayton
Paul Banks of Austin Reed
Bath Museum of Costume
Celia Birtwell
Bloomingdale's (Elizabeth
  Quarta)
Ozwald Boateng
Cavalier Mario Boselli
British Fashion Council
  (Gemma Green)
Camera Nazionale dell'Alta
  Moda Italiana
CDFA
Stephen Chamberlain
Joan Chandler
Christies, for information on
  Henry Price
Ken Clark
Max Clendinning
Clif Colpitts
Angus Cundy of Henry Poole
  and Sons
Daks Simpson
Robert Royal Dawson
Evelyne De Vos Barchman
Jeremy Duncan
Eastman Machine Company
  (Carin Stahlka)

Jo Ellis
Eton Systems (Inger Johansson)
Gordon Ettles
Neri Fadigati of G.B. Giorgini
  Archive
Fashion Monitor (Kieron
  Haycock and Emily Fleuriot)
Fédération Française de la
  Couture du Prêt-à-Porter des
  Couturiers et de Créateurs
  de Mode
FGI
Valerie Figg
Sally Folkes
Fortnum and Mason
Galeries Lafayette
Gerber Technology (Yvonne
  Heinen-Foudeh)
Gieves and Hawkes
Tony Glenville
Nicholas Granger of Norton
  and Sons
Andrew Groves
Shelagh Hancox
Rosemary Harden
Lorraine Harper
Brian Harris
Harrods (Adeline van Roon)
Jenny Hiett
Fiona Hill
Peter Hope Lumley
Gill Huggins
Huntsman
IMB Cologne

Incorporated Society of London
  Fashion Designers
Caroline Irving
Rhian James
Paul Jerome
Paul Jones
Kilgour French & Standbury
Jeff Kwintner
Christian Lacroix
Luton Museum
Macpi
Wendy Malem
Bob Manning
Sheila Mattei
Timothy Morgan-Owen
Ron Pescod of Adeney and
  Boutroy
Première Vision (Christiane de
  Claviere)
Mary Quant (Camilla Twigg)
Zandra Rhodes
Donald Ryding of Glover and
  Ryding
Ann Ryan
Saks of Fifth Avenue
David Sassoon
The Shinn family
John Slater-Dickens
Boris Trambusti
Philip Treacy
Dries Van Noten
Justin Waddell
Sasha Waddell
David Walker

Every effort has been made to identify copyright holders and to acknowledge the source of copyright material. Any inadvertent omissions will be rectified in any future reprinting or edition of this work.

Archery Dress.

An early example of fashion sportswear. Archery became a popular women's sport at the beginning of the 19th century. This fashion plate of 1833 suggests what the fashionable archery devotee should wear.

Introduction

This is not a book about the accepted history of fashion, the psychology of fashion or a chronology of its designers, but how the changes in the processes of manufacture have influenced the evolution of the fashion industry.

A paradoxical industry

There is so much misconception, deliberate and inadvertent misinformation, and ignorance surrounding the world of fashion that it is difficult to get a clear, unbiased picture of how it really works. Information on its levels, operation and terms is essential to an understanding of the subject. This book attempts to remedy this shortcoming. Fashion deals with a world of illusion on the one hand and a hard-bitten, multi-million pound, extremely complex industry on the other. Each aspect relies on the other – the industry needs the fashion illusion to excite the market, and illusion needs the multi-million pound industry to pay for its new ideas, expensive research, extravagance, foibles and design talent.

A complex process

It is because 'the way we look' – our chosen or imagined image – is so important to the human psyche that the illusion aspect of fashion plays, what would seem, such an illogically large role. This, however, is the unstoppable driving force behind that complex process of *design, manufacture* and *distribution* that makes fashion one of the world's most powerful industries.

Design

Design means to have a mental plan, make a preliminary sketch, or delineate an idea or concept in advance of realisation. In the fashion design process this description exactly matches the fashion design activity. The fashion designer conceives the idea, experiments with several alternatives of this idea in sketch form, makes a choice from these, has a pattern cut from this sketch and then has a prototype made up from which a cloth sample can go into manufacture.

Manufacture

This is the process whereby the design is translated into a marketable garment when it is cut, assembled, finished and delivered. This process can be either crafted by hand or mass-produced.

Distribution

This rather unromantic term covers the whole process whereby the goods get to the customer. In fashion this means *selecting* the items from the designer or design manufacturing company and selling or distributing them to the public: in other words this is the transition from wholesale to retail. This process in itself incorporates several sub-processes: *marketing, merchandising, advertising* and *display*.

The levels of the fashion industry

This complex process also operates on different levels: levels of excellence, quality and snobbery. Within the fashion world these levels have acquired names, *couture, ready-to-wear* and *mass production*, and throughout this book these are the terms that will be used to define these levels although it could be argued, for instance, that ready-to-wear is just a form of mass production.

The levels of the fashion industry are really levels of *manufacture*, couture being the highest level and most time-consuming especially in terms of skilled labour, the number of repeat items being only in the tens or twenties. Ready-to-wear or *prêt-à-porter* companies manufacture at a very high level, but industrially and in multiples of hundreds or thousands. Mass production is the cheapest and most highly industrialised and can produce hundreds of thousands to millions of garments.

The history of the three levels is very different. Couture started with the beginning of dressmaking or when the art of constructing garments began – the early medieval *guilds*, the *journeyman* and the seamstress making hand-sewn

PREMET

DRECOLL

The first two scenes from a series of vignettes depicting a visit to the couturier, 'Finishing touches to the new models'. Spring 1924 (designers Premet and Drecoll).

clothes with a needle and thread. In the late 18th century this skill reached such a level of quality and sophistication in the work of court dressmakers such as Rose Bertin and, later, Hippolyte Leroy that the name couture was justified, but it was not until the mid 19th century, when the first *haute couture* house was set up by Charles Frederick Worth in 1858 that the term took on its modern, definitive meaning. Ready-to-wear and mass production had to wait until garment mass production techniques were invented at the end of the 19th century. Ready-to-wear as a high fashion term did not become established until the advent of the *créateurs* in the 1970s.

MARTIAL ET ARMAND

PREMET

The second two scenes in the series 'Finishing touches to the new models'. Spring 1924 (designers Martial et Armand and Premet).

Why the industry divides into these levels

As with most industries, fashion needs innovation to survive and prosper; innovation relies on the inventive and original ideas of designers to prompt change, and change is what keeps the market healthy and interested. The fashion industry is the best example of why the concept of market forces in the manufacturing industries does not, in fact, work. Without the impetus of new ideas, industries like fashion soon shrivel and die. Inventive and original design needs the hotbed environment of the highest level, couture, to nurture its experiments. The second level, ready-to-wear, although also inventive and original, relies on couture to 'soften up' the market and translate avant-garde notions into a truly marketable product. Because fashion is a slow-moving cycle, it is not until several seasons later that the third level, mass production, feeds on, translates and copies the ideas of the two upper levels into products for the mass market.

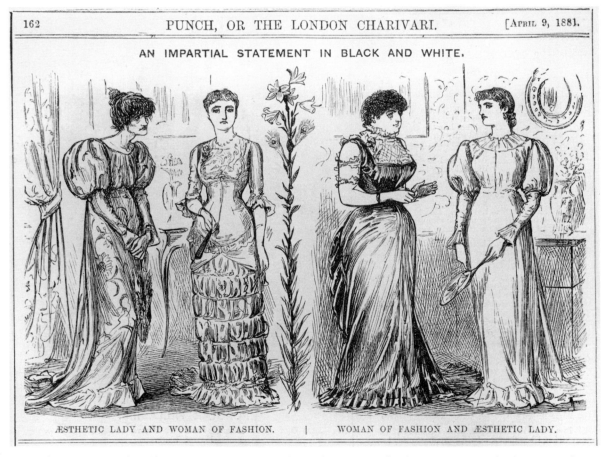

162   PUNCH, OR THE LONDON CHARIVARI.   [April 9, 1881.

AN IMPARTIAL STATEMENT IN BLACK AND WHITE.

ÆSTHETIC LADY AND WOMAN OF FASHION. | WOMAN OF FASHION AND ÆSTHETIC LADY.

'O wad some Power the gift tae gie us, to see oursels as ithers see us' (O that some power had given us the gift to see ourselves as others see us. Robert Burns – 'To a Louse'). The fashionable woman sees herself as perfect and the artistic woman as a scruffy frump, while the artistic woman sees herself as right but the fashionable woman as over-corseted and false: the dichotomy of fashion.

Chapter 1
Couture

Its meaning and place in the fashion industry

The word 'couture' is from the French and means sewing or stitching, so *haute couture* is the high form of this art or craft.

But haute couture means much more. In essence, the difference between haute couture and other forms of manufacturing clothes is that the couture garment is made to the client's individual measurements. This means that the methods of selection are quite different from buying in a retail store – items cannot be selected from *'the rail'* and tried on for shape, colour and size. The couture customer does not know what she will look like in a garment until it is actually completed. Selection for the couture customer is made twice a year, at the spring/summer and autumn/winter *showings* of the *collections*, where prototypes are shown on model girls at a *catwalk show* either in-house or at a particularly fashionable or prestigious venue. Collections comprise a full range of garments, from tailored outerwear to evening dresses, and usually include coats, suits, day dresses, afternoon dresses, cocktail dresses, dinner dresses and ball gowns. The couture client may select several items from the collection where each item is individually named. Names such as 'Bar' and 'Daisy' (1947) or 'Normandie' (1957) at Dior have become famous in the history of fashion as icons of a period or look.

Another area where couture differs from ready-to-wear is the quality of *make* – how well the garment is manufactured. Be it couture or mass production, good or bad, to the discerning eye make is only too evident. In this respect the haute couture garment can be likened to a work of art where every stitch, seam, hem and binding is of superb quality – so perfect that the finished item transcends dressmaking and becomes true craftsmanship. Although made by hand, the couture garment will have all its major seams sewn together by machine, but the finishing – hems, inside seams and linings – are done by hand.

Couture house organisation

The way a couture house is set up, its personnel, its departments and its day-to-day running is entirely based on the Parisian model. The designer or couturier, the *première de l'atelier*, the *seconde*, the *tailleur*, the *flou*, the *directrice* and the *vendeuse* are all members of an established French way of running things taken up by the rest of the world.

The *designer* or *couturier* is the figurehead for the *house*; his or her name is vital to its image. From Charles Frederick Worth in the 1860s to Christian Lacroix today, this fact cannot be

1

Two figured taffetas, strapless evening dresses by Christian Dior, one long and one short, epitomise the ballerina influence of 1954.

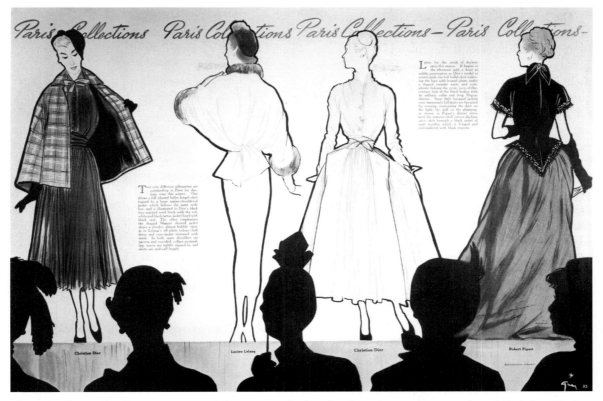

This 1947 illustration by Rene Gruau of the autumn Paris collections shows two examples of Christian Dior's New Look, first shown in the spring of that year. The first left, a checked cape and pleated skirt, and the first right, a dress with bell skirt. It is interesting to note how other designers have already been influenced by Dior – the second on the left is by Lucien Lelong, a Magyar sleeved jacket with a hobble skirt; the second on the right is by Robert Piguet, a dinner dress with a black jacket and immensely full skirt.

overemphasised. Most couturiers have assistant designers but their name is never heard of until they, in turn, set up their own house with their own name. Christian Dior was assistant to Lucien Lelong, Yves Saint Laurent assistant to Christian Dior, Courrèges, Cardin and Ungaro to Balenciaga, and so on.

The designer couturier sets the mood of the house, designs the collections, oversees the toiles, the fittings, chooses the models, arranges the shows, talks to the press, negotiates with backers and takes full responsibility for the house, its reputation and its success. (For a brief biography of the most influential designers see Chapter 8.)

The première de l'atelier is head of the workroom whose job it is to cut the first pattern; make and fit the toile; prepare, cut and fit the garment; and oversee its completion by her workroom hands. The seconde de l'atelier is her second-in-command, and the tailleur, usually a man, has the same job as the première in the tailoring workroom. The flou is in charge of the workroom where bias cut fluid dresses are toiled, cut and made, and the ateliers are the sewing hands or dressmakers.

The *vendeuse* is a high-class saleswoman who arranges for the client to be measured for the items she has selected. If the client is one of long-standing, however, not only will her measurements be known and recorded but also the couture house may have a *dress stand* dedicated to her. The vendeuse in a couture house, although loosely translated as a saleswoman, is a very particular and specialised member of staff. It is through her that the customer will probably have been introduced to the house as each vendeuse has her own list of clients that she alone serves. She oversees the whole process for the client from selection to delivery of the finished garment. She books the *fittings* and liaises with the première or fitter; she will even advise on the selection and suggest items from the collection which she thinks will suit the client and be appropriate to her lifestyle. She will have made it her job to be informed about this and will ensure that two of her clients do not wear the same outfit on the same occasion – the idea that couture items are exclusive to one customer is quite erroneous: a viable number of repeats must be made from each model. Only royalty can ask for the privilege of an exclusive outfit.

For the first fitting the première, who will have measured the client at a previous session, prepares the garment with her assistant in the chosen fabric. It is carefully *tacked* together so that it gives the appearance of a finished garment. The customer will be used to having this construction ripped apart, adjusted, re-marked, re-pinned and refitted until the first stage of the alterations is complete. The garment will then be entirely taken apart, alterations made and the item put together again, bearing in mind all the adjustments made at the first fitting. A second fitting will then be arranged where, hopefully, the fit will be perfect. The garment is now prepared for sewing together, by machine in the case of the major seams and by hand in the case of hems, seam finishes, linings, bindings, pockets and applied decoration. The vendeuse will arrange for the client to have a final fitting where the finished item is tried on and any minor adjustments made. At this point the client will arrange with 'her' vendeuse to take delivery of the garment.

This long and complicated procedure in comparison with trying on an item of clothing in a retail store is one of the disadvantages of haute couture. By the 1970s many younger customers who had money to spend on couture clothes found the whole performance so time-consuming that they welcomed the advent of high quality ready-to-wear clothing. Ready-to-wear was not only instant fashion but also allowed the buyer to try on as many items as they liked and thus select the item that suited them best. Society women often complained of the hours spent at the couturier standing, being fitted and 'having pins stuck in them'.

Couture controlling and supporting bodies

Organisations much like the old guild systems sprang up to regulate the standards, quality and practice of couture houses. The foremost of these and the pattern for the rest of the world is the Chambre Syndicale de la Couture Parisienne based on the house set up by Charles Frederick Worth, 'the first Couturier', in the winter of 1857/58. On this model, similar organisations were set up – in London, the Incorporated Society of London Fashion Designers; in Florence and Rome, the Camera Nazionale dell'Alta Moda Italiana; in New York, the Fashion Group International and the Council of Fashion Designers of America. The strict rules of the Chambre Syndicale, first made in 1945 and updated in 1992, give an idea of the standards that members have to adhere to. To quote the Chambre's own rules, a house 'must employ at least 20 people in its workshops, must present at least 50 designs; day and evening garments to the press during the Spring/Summer and Autumn/ Winter seasons' and 'present the collection to potential clients in the respective couture houses,

Charles Frederick Worth, the father of French haute couture; the Englishman that founded a dynasty of designers and the Chambre Syndicale de la Couture Parisienne in 1868.

in a determined place'. The primary function of these organisations is to promote its members' products by coordinating a calendar of twice-yearly showings (see Chapter 10), liaising with the press and preventing copying. More detailed information on all these organisations can be found in Appendices I to IV.

International couture

Couture was primarily a European practice, and couture houses of different levels and quality flourished in most European capitals. Paris led and the others followed, but Italy, Spain and Britain all had couture designers of note. America, on the other hand, with its vast whole-sale garment-manufacturing base, did not have this tradition and looked to Europe, and especially Paris, for inspiration.

Paris is the recognised home of luxury and perfection: it is no accident that the Englishman Charles Frederick Worth set up his house in Paris. It was the centre for excellence, chic and elegance in style, workmanship and ambience. The highest skilled dressmakers, milliners, embroiderers, belt makers and trimming suppliers were on hand. The luxury and opulence of the great houses from Worth to Chanel and from Dior to Lacroix give Paris the supreme authority in fashion and it is only natural that the Chambre Syndicale should have its home in the heart of Paris in rue du Faubourg Saint Honoré.

Italian couture, probably the most stylish in fashion terms after Paris, operated from three centres – Milan, Florence and Rome – but it is only in Rome, the headquarters of the Camera Nazionale dell'Alta Moda Italiana, its regulating body, that it still flourishes today.

Italy has always had a reputation for high quality luxury fashion goods, and houses such as Sorelle Fontana had been established since the 1930s, but it was not until 1951 that Italian high fashion hit the international market. This was due to the extraordinary enterprise of Marchese Giovanni Battista Giorgini who brought together all the leading Italian couturiers of the day, Simonetta, Fabiani, Sorelle Fontana, Antonelli, Schubert, Carosa, Marucelli, Veneziani, Nobersca, Wanna, Pucci, Galleti, Avolio and Bertoli, in an historic presentation showing in his own house, the Villa Torrigiani, in Florence, to an international audience of fashion press and buyers. This presentation was a huge success and launched Italian couture on to the world stage. Today the records of Giorgini's work can be found in the G.B. Giorgini Archive in Florence.

Spain's fashion style is only too evident in its most famous exports, Cristobal Balenciaga and Antonio Castillo. Balenciaga had a couture house in Saint Sebastian before he opened his Paris house, and Castillo joined the famous old house of Jeanne Lanvin in 1950, which became Lanvin-Castillo. The other Spanish couturiers such as Manuel Pertegaz and Elio Berhanyer

A very good example of how rich Americans patronised Paris couture. The subtlety of the draping on the bodice and sumptuous embroidery on the skirt distinguish this as a model by Worth made for Lady Curzon in 1900. She was the wife of George Curzon, Viscount Scarsdale and Viceroy of India, and the daughter of Levi Ziegler Leiter, founder and proprietor of Marshall Field of Chicago, one of the great department stores of America.

have now been largely forgotten by the international market, but in the 1950s and 1960s, top fashion magazines featured their collections each season along with those of Paris, London, Rome and New York.

British couture, never really as stylish as French or Italian, had a particular English elegance based on its clientele, the English upper classes, whose penchant for hunting and hunt balls meant that its tailoring was immaculate and its ball gowns spectacular. Hardy Amies, Charles Creed, Michael and Digby Morton were the great tailors, and Norman Hartnell, Bianca Mosca, Victor Stiebel and John Cavanagh created romantic ball gowns (see Appendix I).

Although Germany is the biggest manufacturer of fashion clothing in Europe it has never really made its mark in haute couture. Not until today with the brilliant Jil Sander or the innovative Helmut Lang (an Austrian, of course) have German designers had any impact on world fashion and both Sander and Lang are primarily ready-to-wear designers.

With its huge wholesale garment manufacturing base and its highly sophisticated marketing techniques, American couture has always tended to be a halfway house between couture and ready-to-wear. This approach has spawned many great designers but not really couturiers, with the notable exception of the genius Charles James, the international Mainbocher, and America's great classicist, Norman Norell (see Chapter 8). America always looked to Paris for inspiration and through its press and extraordinary buying power was probably Paris's greatest supporter. Lately, by a strange twist of fate, several American designers have taken over at famous French houses – Tom Ford at Yves Saint Laurent, Oscar de la Renta at Pierre Balmain and Mark Jacobs at Louis Vuitton.

Right: this drawing taken from a sketch from the Creed archive shows a suit designed for the celebrated World War I spy Mata Hari. It was always maintained by the staff at Charles Creed that she was in fact shot in a Creed suit in 1917.

Hardy Amies, the Queen's couturier and founder member of the Incorporated Society of London Fashion Designers, with Lady Pamela Berry, president of the Society from 1954 to 1960.

Paris couture houses

In Paris the couture houses were huge and their influence immense. Paris dominated world fashion for a century, from 1860 to 1960. No self-respecting American millionaire's wife would consider buying her wardrobe anywhere but Paris. Even in the 19th century, Americans were buying 'models' in Paris and copying them back home either under licence or illegally. This practice was not confined to America – London court dressmakers bought Paris models to copy, as did dressmakers and gown manufacturers in the other capitals of Europe. Paris couturiers used the 'insurance' of their worldwide fame to set up branches in other cities, for example Worth in London and Molyneux in London, Biarritz and Cannes.

The most celebrated women of the day patronised particular Parisian couturiers – European royalty had their clothes made in Paris and even Queen Victoria is reputed to have had her clothes from Worth in Paris but delivered through the London branch so as not to appear unpatriotic. Society women, actresses and even well-known courtesans not only patronised certain couturiers but might also, if they were particularly elegant or beautiful, be used as *mannequin de ville*, that is provided with free wardrobes in order to wear them in public and, in modern terms, 'advertise' them at social events such as the races and balls. Sarah Bernhardt, the great French actress, dressed at Worth; the spy Mata Hari had her suits made at Creed; and the celebrated comedienne Réjane patronised Doucet.

In order to provide for this vast market the couture houses were in themselves vast and employed large numbers of workers. At its height, the house of Worth employed more than one thousand.

London couture houses

Even in London, from the early 1920s to the mid 1960s, couture houses were very large establishments, some employing hundreds of staff, from the directrice, the several vendeuses, their assistants and the secretaries at the front of the house, to the substantial workrooms at the back where fitters, dressmakers, tailors and dress hands worked unseen by the customers. There would be at least two large dress workrooms, a tailoring workroom and a skirt workroom. Each workroom would house up to twenty experienced *hands*, their juniors, assistants and apprentices. The workroom was run by the all-powerful fitters who modelled the patterns in mull or calico on the stand, made the toiles and did all the fittings, liaising with the designer for the first models (or prototypes) and with the vendeuses when the customer had the model made to her size. In the 1950s, Norman Hartnell employed 385 staff at his house at 36 Bruton Street. His workers, like other London couture house employees, worked a 41 hour week on a very limited wage often as little as thirty shillings (£1.50) a week for the most junior to five pounds ten shillings (£5.50) per week for a top rate hand, whilst male tailors could earn in excess of six pounds per week and all were entitled to a holiday of one working day for each month of the year worked. The directrice, the vendeuses or their assistants, who worked on a commission basis and would have brought their own set of customers with them, were considered to be in a different social class from the workroom staff and were able to negotiate their own salaries.

Pages 9 and 10 show the work of members of the Incorporated Society of London Fashion Designers: Left: navy wool coat by Edward Molyneux 1948. Right: tweed top coat by Hardy Amies 1950.

Left: black silk evening dress by Bianca Mosca 1949.
Right: tulle ball dress by Norman Hartnell 1953.

From the G.B. Giorgini Archive representing the Camera Nazionale dell'Alta Moda Italiana.

Left: an evening dress by Antonelli 1955 in the Sala Bianca, Pitti Palace, Florence.

Below: an evening dress by Fabiani 1951.

Dame Margot Fonteyn, the prima ballerina, was a good advertisement for haute couture – she bought from both London and Paris. These five dresses, part of her French wardrobe, are by Yves Saint Laurent and are in the Bath Museum of Costume.

Hollywood and haute couture

In the 1930s and 1940s the public's perception of fashion was mostly through the medium of Hollywood films. Many women could describe in detail what Greta Garbo wore in a particular scene, the cut of a Jean Harlow gown or Rita Hayworth's famous dress in *Gilda*. Others, who could afford it, would ask their local dressmaker to copy dresses from the latest film magazines. But unknown to the general filmgoing public, all these much-publicised garments were designed and made by couturiers. The great film costume designers Adrian, Travis Banton, Orry Kelly and Edith Head had nearly all trained as couturiers before going into films and had run their own couture houses – some had even worked in Paris with the great couturiers of the day. Therefore a bias cut satin sheath worn by Jean Harlow was in fact an adaptation of a Madeleine Vionnet expertly reinvented by Adrian, the doyen of the Hollywood costume designers. The 1939 film *The Women* was a tour de force exposition of the American woman featuring no fewer than six Hollywood stars including Joan Crawford, Rosalind Russell and Norma Shearer. Each character was supposedly dressed by a different Paris couturier; they were all in fact designed by Adrian. The public in this period were almost subliminally influenced by French haute couture ideals.

The decline of the couture system in the 1960s

It was really in London that the 1960s fashion revolution began. Mary Quant has been credited

This advertisement from *Woman's Journal* of July 1946, featuring dresses by Hattie Carnegie and Adele Simpson, is a good example of the overlap between couture and ready-to-wear in the American market. Both Carnegie and Simpson were in the highest echelons of American fashion, but used ready-to-wear methods to manufacture their garments. Carnegie was one of the doyennes of American high fashion; Claire McCardell and Norman Norell worked for and learned their craft from her.

with bringing about this phenomenon but it was not, of course, just Mary Quant; London's fashion revolution was a revolution in thought, style and behaviour and was the complete antithesis of the strict rules of the Chambre Syndicale or the Incorporated Society of London Fashion Designers. Music, art, theatre and sexual liberation were the stimuli for this dynamic movement.

Before 1960, fashion standards had been set by the rich and sophisticated – the 'older woman' if not actually older, looked older and was certainly very sophisticated and the ideal to which all fashion aspirants aimed. Even young fashion students in art schools were designing cocktail dresses, dinner dresses and ball gowns, clothes for events that most had never been to and for a society of which most of them had no knowledge. The young were still dressed either as 'jeune filles' by their mothers – a parody of the debutante dress – or in exactly the same way as their mothers.

Because this revolution took place in the London of the Swinging Sixties, the contrast between the couturiers of the Incorporated Society and what was happening in the street became even more marked. Young couture designers of the day no longer wanted to be associated with the staid style of the Incorporated Society – David Sassoon, designer at Belinda Bellville, London's youngest and most successful couture house of the mid 1960s, turned down the offer of membership. Belinda Bellville, later Bellville Sassoon, was the only couture house in London to meet the challenge of the Swinging Sixties. It was around the corner from the King's Road, Chelsea, and as David Sassoon says, 'we needed to bring the fun and excitement of what was happening on the streets on to the catwalk'.

Janey Ironside, touted by the press of the day as 'the first professor of fashion' at the Royal College of Art, transformed the fashion school there into a seed-bed for young fashion talent, and Muriel Pemberton at St Martin's School of Art, always a nurturer of the eccentric, bred a rival team of budding fashion talent. These young designers set their sights not towards the established couture world but towards the more immediate and accessible wholesale fashion market. By the late 1960s, especially with the advent of the Beatle's *Sergeant Pepper* album which set the seal on the hippie movement, all kinds of second-hand clothing were, for a time, the main element of dress for the young, fashionable set. The army greatcoat, the frogged jacket, Afghan furs, old silk pyjamas became the staple diet of the trendsetters. Design companies then began to incorporate these items and this feeling into their collections.

Paris was much slower to take up these ideas and with great difficulty acquiesced to the 'London scene'. It was perhaps this short-lived London supremacy in fashion that was most influential in making ready-to-wear the vehicle through which high fashion operated from this point onwards.

The seeds of the Swinging Sixties were sown in the late 1950s, when beatnik art students' culture demanded a breaking down of traditional values, which included dress. On a different social scale, mods (of the mods and rockers street movement) were another precursor of 1960s style. Short, crisp wind-cheaters, narrow trousers, desert boots, short, neat hair characterised the men, and a short bob, short skirts, low-heeled shoes and a slouching stance typified the girls.

These mods, who travelled in packs on scooters, were a British phenomenon. Particularly dress conscious, they became another model from which 1960s fashion and iconoclasm sprang. Why did this happen in Britain? From an early period, Britain has been famous for producing eccentrics and dress eccentricities – even Marie-Antoinette, the arbiter of French taste before the Revolution, fell in love with this quirky English look, and the casual, almost throwaway style of the romantic Gainsborough portraits became the model for the French queen's entourage (see also Chapter 4).

As so often happens with an embattled group, the couture establishment clung on too hard to their principles and, by the natural process of fashion, became out of date. In London, except in very few greatly reduced couture houses, couture-made clothes died out. Their customers with a now outmoded lifestyle of hunting, racing, regattas, garden parties, cocktail parties, formal dinners and balls were part of the old guard. The British Labour prime minister Harold Wilson and his government courted the Beatles and successfully degraded the old aristocracy, the backbone of London couture.

In Paris it was a different story: the couturiers took on the 1960s looks. André Courrèges, a rival contender to Mary Quant as the inventor of the mini skirt, Emanuel Ungaro, Paco Rabanne and Pierre Cardin each built their reputation on space-age couture-constructed versions of what in London was street wear. The immaculate hand finish of these garments was somehow a paradox. Ready-to-wear was the most appropriate method of construction for this particular look – the designers needed the mass production manufacturing techniques to give them the crispness they required. Thirty years earlier, the Bauhaus designers had designed expressly for mass production to enhance the look of their product. Conversely, the couture designers of the 1960s detracted from their style with inappropriate hand finishes.

By the 1970s, Paris couture was only for the super-rich, and many of these clients were South American women and the wives of New York millionaires, who still preferred Paris couture. These women were inevitably the not so young: establishment figures who dressed to suit their husbands and their somewhat staid tastes. The keynote of 1960s and 1970s fashion was youth, and inevitably those couture houses catering primarily for the wealthy, older clients could not afford to indulge in this look which was consequently and eagerly taken up by the créateurs or ready-to-wear designers.

Pant suit by André Courrèges of 1964 from his famous, revolutionary space-age collection heralding an entirely new look in couture.

It has been said that a fashion designer can expect only ten years at the top. This peculiarity, exacerbated by the death of Dior and Balenciaga and the decline of Patou, Ricci, Lanvin, Grès and, by the late 1970s, Cardin and Courrèges, spelt the end of Paris couture in its accepted form – even the great Saint Laurent preferred his Rive Gauche ready-to-wear range to his couture collections at this period.

Another factor in the decline of couture was the difficulty of acquiring sufficiently skilled dressmakers, tailors and sewing hands to produce the clothes – as early as the 1950s the shortage of skilled labour had taxed the ingenuity of the Incorporated Society of London Fashion Designers. One of the recurrent worries, voiced at the meetings of the Society, was how to recruit, train and encourage young people to take up work or join apprenticeship schemes in the poorly paid couture workrooms. Those who had done their apprenticeships in the 1930s were now reaching retirement age and were not able or inclined to pass on their skills to a largely indifferent workforce. Wages had to increase to a reasonable level but this meant that the true cost of a couture garment was finally realised. To the average customer this cost seemed astronomical. The mass production manufacturing methods used by both the ready-to-wear and mass production industries could ensure a living wage for the operatives and a competitive price to the customer. Thus from every side the sometime bastion of fashion, haute couture, was being eclipsed by its younger and cheaper rival, ready-to-wear.

The upkeep of the large and luxurious 'houses' in the smartest areas of town also became prohibitive – many couturiers, unlike their American rivals in ready-to-wear, had received no training in business and had no idea how much their establishments actually cost.

The decline in the market, the scarcity of properly trained workers and the prohibitive expense of centrally placed and luxurious premises meant that those who did still want to buy and wear made-to-measure clothes started to look elsewhere. Many designers who could still call on and employ skilled dressmakers looked to this new, smaller market. By working from home or a small studio and visiting and fitting clients in their own homes they found they could conduct a perfectly viable dressmaking business. On the whole this business concentrated on bridal, bridesmaid and mother-of-the-bride outfits. These new establishments called themselves couturiers but were really dressmakers and would never have passed the rigorous tests for quality, originality and exclusivity set by the Chambre Syndicale or the Incorporated Society of London Fashion Designers. In many ways this new development tarnished the name of couture.

The revival of couture in the 1980s and 1990s

The so-called power dressing of the 1980s was the manifestation of a new role for women in the business and professional world. The new woman was her own boss, had plenty of money to spend and used fashion to express her new-found strength. No longer the accessory to her male partner or an expression of his wealth and status, this woman could please herself and did so, and spent a lot of money on clothes. The success of ready-to-wear companies like Donna Karan, Giorgio Armani, Ralph Lauren and Gianni Versace is proof of this phenomenon. But these clothes, with their success, became more and more expensive and these astute businesswomen with their own money to spend discovered that a couture dress was not that much more expensive than a dress at the top end of the ready-to-wear market. Gianfranco Ferre at Dior, Yves Saint Laurent, Gianni Versace and the newly opened Christian Lacroix were now comparatively affordable.

This boom made couture houses hot property and the conglomerates moved in. Huge cosmetic companies started buying houses – Charles of the Ritz bought Yves Saint Laurent, for example.

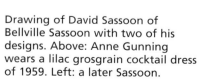

Drawing of David Sassoon of Bellville Sassoon with two of his designs. Above: Anne Gunning wears a lilac grosgrain cocktail dress of 1959. Left: a later Sassoon.

Fashion's status moved higher and higher in the finance markets. Jockeying for places in this new, global, high finance fashion market meant that design companies had to have higher and higher profiles. When Chanel took on Karl Lagerfeld and so successfully turned round that business which, since Chanel's death in 1971, had been in decline, the business fashion world took note. A brilliant designer with a high profile, a brilliant publicity campaign and an ego to match could transform a failing once-famous company and, more importantly, revitalise all its subsidiaries – scent, cosmetics, hosiery, jewellery, bags, accessories and, above all, designer jeans. This example became the model for other conglomerates with fashion ambitions. Christian Dior and Givenchy took on John Galliano, a brilliant but comparatively inexperienced designer, who had left St Martin's School of Art in the 1980s. In 1997 Galliano then moved to Dior and his place at Givenchy was taken over by an even less experienced designer, Alexander McQueen, another St Martin's graduate. These appointments had exactly the desired effect: heightening the profile of each house. The publicity became phenomenal and the sales of the subsidiary products increased proportionally. Whether the clothes sold is another matter, but this was not the point of this particular exercise.

Making techniques and their influence on fashion

The make or construction techniques employed in garment assembly have been a crucial factor in the development and evolution of fashion. Each major fashion change has brought about a revolution in the way clothes are constructed. The corset and the hoop, in one form or another, had been the basis of so much of women's fashion

Right: Gabrielle Chanel's third incarnation, but designed by Karl Lagerfeld who took over the house in 1983 and gave it a third lease of life. This brilliant denim skirted update is from 1991.

Christian Lacroix's haute couture outfit from the spring/summer 1993 collection.

Above: photograph of Christian
Lacroix by Guido Mocafico.

Right: bead embroidered outfit
from Christian Lacroix's
autumn/winter 1998/99 collection.

20

until the beginning of the 20th century. Ousted for a short period from 1785 to 1820 by free flowing, figure-revealing dresses, it returned in full-blown form in the mid 19th century with the constrictions of the crinoline. So many fashion innovations were built on this highly constructed foundation, and it was not until Paul Poiret introduced the apparently unstructured tea gown that this rigid structural formula was abandoned.

The movement towards informality in dress that characterises the 20th century, in theory, threw out the corset and the hoop. Through Poiret's tea gown in the early years of the 20th century, to the simple camisole shifts of the 1920s, to the 'invention' of the bias cut by Madeleine Vionnet in the 1930s, softness and fluidity in women's clothing reached its apogee. When film stars like Jean Harlow said, 'I wear nothing under this', they were being practical rather than provocative. To wear anything at all under a bias cut evening gown would be only too evident, revealing the unsightly bumps and lumps of any underpinnings.

The influence of World War II uniforms and the effect of rationing reintroduced some of the sharper techniques of tailoring. Dior's New Look in 1947, however, revolutionised making and construction. Corsets were back, as were all the many variations of interlining and mounting, and the volume of cloth used, to the horror of politicians, was on a par with that used in an 1860s crinoline. The dichotomy between constructed and non-constructed has been a constant theme over the past twenty years – Sonia Rykiel's soft cardigans could not be more different from Jean-Paul Gaultier's *bustiers*.

Characteristics and specialities of fitters

Each première or fitter is known to the designer for special qualities – an ability to drape chiffon, achieve a generous shape or being particularly good at waisted or tight fitting garments. One that is good at one look will not necessarily be good at another. Part of the designer's art is to pick the fitter most appropriate to a new style. Fitters, tailors and cutters can be staid in their ideas, however clever: to persuade a fitter that a tight-fitting suit jacket does not need ease can be difficult; likewise, when narrow fitting shapes are current it is difficult to persuade the same fitter to get a new feeling for volume. Nevertheless, it is part of the designer's job to persuade and cajole his team. Established cutting and construction techniques die hard with most technical experts but it is often the breaking of the rules that achieves a new look – it is these new silhouettes or changes in cut that identify the avant-garde.

Couture today

Couture has become so tied up in the branding game that it is difficult to tell how many of the houses operate today in the traditional way. Some, like Christian Lacroix and Emanuel Ungaro, continue to function as they have always done – and of course have their ready-to-wear outlets to boost sales. But the giants like Christian Dior, Givenchy and Versace appear now to use their couture collections merely as showcases for their other products: jeans, scent and accessories. It is difficult to see how couture customers would be influenced by actresses wearing particular outfits at the Oscar Academy Awards ceremony in Hollywood. Such events will of course affect designer jeans and in some cases designer ready-to-wear sales but not to a noticeable degree the sophisticated couture client.

The effect of the latest movement in couture has been to blur the edges: when Anna Wintour of *American Vogue* cites haute couture as the avant-garde in today's fashion it is difficult to tell who is influencing whom. Does the new couture really influence the top end of the ready-to-wear market? Surely not, as the créateurs designers are already the trendsetters. Does couture influence the high street? The answer to this is probably yes: with shorter and shorter lead times, an idea from Galliano's Dior catwalk show can be in the high street within a few weeks.

K.351

L.211

F.180

'Nicoll Clothes'
41-45 Warwick Street, W.I
Telephone : Regent 1951

Coat, suit and tailored dress *ca.* 1940 from Nicoll Clothes, women's tailored ready-mades with a retail shop in London's Regent Street.

Chapter 2
Ready-to-Wear

Definition – Origins of ready-to-wear – The evolution of ready-to-wear – Utility Clothing – Fashion revolution in London in the 1960s – The influence of the 1960s revolution on Paris – Design process – Ready-to-wear manufacturing techniques – Ready-to-wear workrooms or studios – Factors in the growth of the ready-to-wear industry – The regulating or supporting bodies – Ready-to-wear versus haute couture – The Japanese influence – The emergence of Belgium – Italy's role in ready-to-wear – British ready-to-wear – America: the first in ready-to-wear

Definition

The terms *ready-to-wear, prêt-à-porter* or *off-the-peg* are comparatively new and describe a method of buying clothes whereby the customer no longer has to have clothes *made to measure* – that time-consuming method that involves choosing a style, selecting a cloth, being measured, having a series of fittings and, finally, several weeks later, taking delivery of the garment (see Chapter 1). Buying ready-to-wear means that the customer can select garments, already in their size, direct from the *dress rail*, try them on, discard any styles that do not suit or fit, and know, most importantly of all, exactly what he or she looks like in the garment there and then. The problem with this method is that items have to be made in many different sizes, and the retail outlet, be it boutique, department store or *concession shop*, has to keep a large stock of items from which the customer can make a choice. (It is from this function of holding stock or storing sufficient numbers, *colourways* and sizes that the use of the word *store* arose – see Glossary.) Ready-to-wear also involves complicated sizing problems and manufacture in large quantities. It uses, of course, the same basic manufacturing methods as mass production but the term 'ready-to-wear' (RTW) has come to mean the more exclusive *designer end* of the market. Today it is the major area in which named designers operate other than in couture.

Origins of ready-to-wear

It has been commonly said that ready-to-wear was born as a result of World War I uniform manufacturers devising new methods of mass-producing uniforms for the millions of soldiers sent to the trenches in Belgium and northern France in 1914–18. The *trench coat* and *battle dress* are examples of new items of clothing based on these uniforms. Previously, tailors had made uniforms for the officer class to whom those uniforms had been a matter of great pride and one of the items of expenditure that an officer and gentleman had to budget for.

But ready-to-wear has much earlier antecedents – *la confection*, the original French term for ready-to-wear, helps put it in its proper context. In France the word 'confection' is still used to denote the *wholesale dress industry*. La confection started in the late 18th century when second-hand clothes dealers also stocked unwanted samples from tailors and dressmakers. This could be their residue stock or items that

These 'washing frocks' from John Lewis, May 1932, are inexpensive and very stylish but must owe their existence to the great Paris couturier Edward Molyneux.

Compare the images on p. 24 with these that he designed for Gertrude Lawrence in Noel Coward's *Private Lives* in the year before.

the made-to-measure customer had not paid for or collected. A particular stall in Marché Saint Jacques in Paris became so popular for this new merchandise that tailors and dressmakers produced and supplied items just to sell in this manner, and the centre for this new rag trade was born. Milliners, who sold many more items than just hats, such as petticoats, trimmings, ribbons, frills, flounces and bodices that could be assembled to make an outfit, were in many ways selling a form of ready-to-wear separates. Even the description of Rose Bertin's shops in the 1780s makes this obvious – millinery was almost a generic term for the general professional dressmaker. In Wilkie Collins' *Armadale*, set in about 1860, Lydia Gwilt calls at the 'milliner' to order some cheap dresses.

For so many years ready-to-wear, or the wholesale dress industry as it was then called, the poor relation of haute couture, took its lead from its aristocratic cousin until the advent of the créateurs in the mid 1970s. Until this time, all wholesale or ready-to-wear clothing was based on what was happening in couture and more especially what was happening in Paris haute couture. The lengths that wholesale dress manufacturers, especially the Americans, would go to to copy a new Paris style were often the stuff of many a good press story. However apocryphal these stories might be, a huge amount of illegal copying did take place and the inspiration of the work of the great couturiers is only too obvious in the ready-to-wear styles of the day. Official copies sanctioned by the couturier were a method of making money for the great designers; in fact part of the original brief of the Chambre Syndicale for their designers was to produce *models* from which the wholesale dress industry could make copies in volume.

The evolution of ready-to-wear

Ready-to-wear is a type of mass production, which had become mechanised in the middle of the 19th century with the invention of the sewing machine when it was more familiarly known as *ready-mades*. It is perhaps ironic that the Honourable Daisy Fellows, the first president of the Incorporated Society of London Fashion Designers, that bastion of British haute couture, was the granddaughter of Winnaretta Singer, the sewing machine inventor's daughter. According to Winifred Aldrich, the practice of manufacturing multiples in clothing started much earlier (Aldrich, 2000). Other mass production techniques – production lines, multiple copies, and volume production so evident in the other industries in the nineteenth century – took much longer to become established in the dress industry. This may have been due to the fact that the cutting, making and assembly of a garment that fits all sizes posed many more problems. Advertisements were, however, to be seen in women's magazines as early as the 1890s for ready-made items – 'The best 10/6 costume of the season' in *Weldon Ladies Journal*. Ten shillings and sixpence, just over 50 pence, for a whole costume with tailored jacket and floor-length flared skirt, indicated that it must have been manufactured in bulk to achieve the price.

The conversion of traditional crafts into mechanised mass production methods was the preoccupation of all industry during the Industrial Revolution, and by the end of the 19th century a myriad of consumer items were designed, manufactured and distributed to the public and exported to all corners of the globe. Although some industries changed their design methods to fit these new manufacturing techniques, the dress trade always aped the upper end of the market, haute couture. By the beginning of the 20th century, in Germany the Bauhaus movement deliberately incorporated these newly invented production techniques at the design stage, thus expressing their new and seemingly revolutionary design philosophy, 'form follows function'.

It was both the complicated series of stages that dress manufacture had to go through, from idea to finished garment, and the problem of

Advertisement from *Weldon Ladies Journal* of 1899 for a two-piece costume for only ten shillings and sixpence – just over 50 pence. A good example of a 'ready-made' in the 19th century.

Utility Clothing

In Britain, many lessons in economy of material and process were learned in World War II as a result of the introduction of Utility Clothing. In 1942, the president of the Incorporated Society of London Fashion Designers, the Honourable Daisy Fellows, thought the Society should 'identify with the National Effort' and thus the Utility Clothing Scheme was born. Delegates from the Society met officials from the Board of Trade at Millbank House to discuss an 'Outline for Utility Clothing'. The constraints put on the clothing industry by this regime sharpened the inventive powers of the industry's managers and encouraged them to develop new ideas in use of cloth, economy of labour, and ultra practical designing techniques. The post-war dress industry was thus modernised and, with a huge emphasis on exports, new markets opened up especially in America. These American markets became the target for most post-war European dress manufacturers.

Fashion revolution in London in the 1960s

As explained in the previous chapter, it was not really until the fashion revolution in London in the 1960s that ready-to-wear emerged as the chief exponent of high fashion. Until this point it had been the poor relation and certainly kept in its place by the all-powerful couture establishment. In 1948, Frederick Starke, representing the London Model House Group of ready-to-wear companies, approached the Incorporated Society of London Fashion Designers about a meeting to discuss a possible tie-up between the Society and the Group. The Model House Group was firmly rebuffed: 'this meeting not encouraged by members'.

The development of ready-to-wear varies in different countries and springs from quite different roots. In Europe, ready-to-wear developed from the boutiques of the couture houses where

sizing that held back high quality mass production in the dress and tailoring trades. The journey from idea to final finished garment is certainly as complex as producing a motor car. A garment first has to have a pattern; this then has to be marked out on the fabric, before being cut out. When cut out the pieces have to be *bundled*, *docketed* and then sewn together. After this the finishing process takes place – hemming, lining and sewing on trims and buttons. When, in the past, only one operator, the dressmaker, performed all these functions the process was relatively easy, but when each process has to be completed and operated separately as in mass production, the sequence of functions becomes particularly complicated.

These model dresses from Debenham and Freebody dated 1939 could not have been inspired by any other designer than the inimitable Elsa Schiaparelli. The silhouette, funnel hats and diagonal embroidery show how successfully couture designers' ideas were translated into the ready-to-wear market.

Three real Schiaparellis of January 1938 clearly showing the influence for the Debenham and Freebody models.

UTILITY

CC41

Above: Utility Clothing was introduced in 1942 through the collaboration of the Board of Trade and the Incorporated Society of London Fashion Designers. The initiative produced some very well designed clothes and the well-known symbol as seen in the picture.

Right: Suit by Dorville, May 1948, typical of good quality women's fashion wholesale tailoring of the period.

at first they sold accessories, scarves, jewellery and scent. This progressed into selling items of clothing that could be bought directly over the counter: no ordering, no fittings – 'off the peg'. In America, where the ready-to-wear market had been much more sophisticated from an early period, the huge New York Seventh Avenue *rag trade* developed.

The ready-to-wear designers of the London fashion boom were mostly graduates of the British art schools. Mary Quant who, it is often reported, denied having a formal training in fashion, in fact studied at London's Goldsmith's College of Art where she met Alexander Plunket Greene whom she married in 1957 and together they set up Bazaar, a shop in the King's Road of seminal importance to British fashion and the start of her fashion empire. Another husband and wife team Barbara Hulanicki and Stephen Fitz-Simon opened Biba in Abingdon Road, Kensington, in 1963. From this sprang another empire and another huge influence on British lifestyle: everyone from Twiggy to Mick Jagger wore Biba T-shirts, boots, satin suits and floppy hats. After this a spate of designer shops sprang up, where the designers were Royal College or St Martin's graduates: Jim O'Connor and Pam Harvey at Mr Freedom, Bus Stop with Lee Bender, Sally Tuffin and Marion Foale at Foale and Tuffin, James Wedge at Count Down, Stirling Cooper (where Anthony Price, Alice Pollock and Shelagh Brown were the designers), Ossie Clark at Quorum, and Zandra Rhodes and Sylvia Ayton with the Fulham Road Clothes Shop. Names like Hung On You, Granny Takes a Trip and Sex gave the psychedelic flavour to an era that was certainly heavily influenced by drugs. Designers like Jean Muir, Bill Gibb, John Bates, Gina Fratini, Bruce Oldfield, Janice Wainright, Wendy Dagworthy and the inimitable Vivienne Westwood in all her many reincarnations gave London the edge.

The influence of swinging London, and in particular King's Road, Chelsea, and Carnaby Street, on world fashion cannot be overestimated; the buzz, the excitement and the raw creativity, as London showed off and the rest of the world observed, were all-pervasive. Not only was every fashion celebrity on the streets but photographers and fashion press were also there to record and take part in this prodigious happening.

The influence of the 1960s revolution on Paris

As outlined in the previous chapter, Paris was slow in responding to the London scene; the Paris créateurs came from a rather different background – most had trained at the Chambre Syndicale school and been apprentices or assistants to the great couturiers. Karl Lagerfeld, always a rival to Yves Saint Laurent, was assistant to Pierre Balmain, while Saint Laurent was at Dior. Lagerfeld then went on to Chloé, where he made his name and later became one of France's most prolific designers. Emmanuelle Khan, a model for Balenciaga and Givenchy, worked first for Cacharel before setting up her own business in 1963. Daniel Hechter began working with Pierre D'Alby and made a huge impact on all levels of ready-to-wear in France, and Sonia Rykiel, unbelievably untrained, started on her own in 1962. Kenzo at Jap and Issey Miyake, both Japanese, had Parisian training – Kenzo selling designs to Feraud in 1970 and Miyake working for Guy Laroche after studying fashion at the Chambre Syndicale school. The other Japanese designers who had a huge impact on Paris ready-to-wear were Rei Kawakubo at Comme des Garçons and Yohji Yamamoto. (This phenomenal Japanese influence is described in detail later in the chapter.) A new wildness was brought to Paris by a fresh burst of French talent in the 1970s with Claude Montana, Thierry Mugler and Jean-Paul Gaultier who, in particular, had been influenced by the London scene of the 1960s.

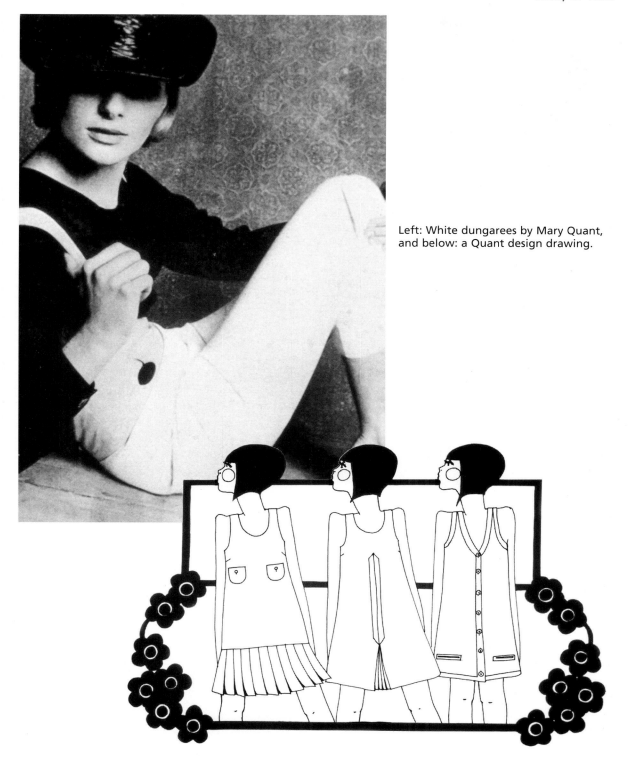

Left: White dungarees by Mary Quant, and below: a Quant design drawing.

Left: Mary Quant's 1967 'Banana Split' dress modelled by Grace Coddington.

Below: A portrait of Quant in 1960.

34

Ideas that influenced a generation,
from Ossie Clark's sketchbooks from
the late 1960s.

Above: a portrait of Zandra Rhodes in 1972 by Robin Beeche with make-up by Yvonne Gold.

Right: Four outfits from Rhodes' 1977 'Mexican' collection. Photograph by Clive Arrowsmith.

These designs by Gina Fratini are typical of the 1960s. It is a drawing style made popular by Barbara Hulanicki.

The whole lid black. False eyelashes (Triple thickness). heavily mascarared but straight — not curly. Palest pink (almost white with a pink tinge.)

Hair Vidal Sasoon.

nail varnish very silvet pink. again almost white.

navy blue. Shoes Arnello + Davide.

Right: this drawing worksheet from 1965, by John Bates, shows how the designer thinks out not only the design but also how it will be presented: hairstyle, make-up, in fact the total look.

Below: Part of the Japanese influence. This new take on a shirt-waister dress by Kenzo for Jap, 1977, epitomises the easy but revolutionary cutting that the Japanese designers brought to Paris.

Above: Karl Lagerfeld for Chloe: a printed dress of 1981, before his move to Chanel, worn here by Lady Silvy Thynne.

Design process

The design is conceived by the designer or the design team. For each design many *roughs* have to be sketched, discussed, selected, modified, finalised and drawn up. Some designers like one design drawing to say everything: 'a working drawing with a highly illustrative content', as Sylvia Ayton, the design director of Wallis, so aptly put it. Other designers prefer to make a more conceptual sketch from which they then have to make a detailed working or specification drawing to ensure that the pattern cutter can understand exactly what the designer has in mind. Others find it more helpful to drape on the stand, conceiving an idea in the round.

Whichever method the designer uses, he/she must have inspiration or a theme to build ideas around. For this inspiration the designer seeks out different sources of reference: a trip to a remote island or absorbing a new culture, museum visits to view specific items or to look at the work of contemporary or past painters. Most designers find that to fully take in the reference they have found they need to make colour or drawn studies, usually in a sketchbook. It may take several attempts to find the right theme for that season, as originality at this stage is vital to generating ideas. These ideas need to be ideas of silhouette, colour, texture, cut and fabric. As many as fifty ideas may be generated before one final design is decided upon.

Range building is an important part of the designer's repertoire. A range is a small, linked group of garments that need to compliment each other from a buying point of view. A range of dresses, for example, needs to include a short-sleeved dress, a long-sleeved dress, a sleeveless dress, a dress with a high neckline, a dress with a low neckline and perhaps a dress with a boat-shaped neckline. A range of separates, on the other hand, must coordinate – several tops must be able to go with several bottoms. Often, three items in a range can be worn together, and a good designer knows that a completely disparate piece will be left on the rail and end up in the sale.

Another of the designer's responsibilities is cloth selection which is made right at the beginning of the design process, in February/March for spring/summer of the following year, and September for the following autumn/winter. This vital and difficult practice takes place at one of the international cloth fairs such as Première Vision in Paris and Moda In in Milan (see Chapter 10).

Ready-to-wear manufacturing techniques

The manufacturing techniques of ready-to-wear are basically the same as mass production but demand a higher quality of make. This demand can lead to problems for the design company because the quantities within which they work, in comparison with those of the huge mass production companies, are very small. Production companies and *outwork factories* with the latest technology want orders from companies that demand high output or *volume* in order to make their investment in the new technology pay. High fashion design companies therefore, ironically, have to use much smaller, less well-equipped and not necessarily very up-to-date outwork manufacturers.

Ready-to-wear workrooms or studios

The ready-to-wear workroom has, in many ways, greater links with the old couture *atelier* or workroom. Because the designer, sample pattern cutter and sample machinist need to work closely, the ready-to-wear workroom has an atmosphere rather like that of a studio. There can, of course, be several sample pattern cutters and several sample machinists. Each of these operatives is an expert in their field with a high degree of input into how the technical design problems of each garment should be solved.

Because of its character, the ready-to-wear workroom can be comparatively small and thus located in a central, urban position. Although the overheads may be high, the design workroom needs to be near the city centre to operate efficiently. It will often include a showroom where samples can be shown to the press, *buyers* and outworkers. For this, a model can be employed on an hourly basis during the showing season – February/March and September/October – much like the in-house shows at a couture house but on a less ambitious scale. The model will also be employed during the sample-making period, just prior to showing, to enable the designer and cutter to fit, adjust and modify the sample garment.

It takes about six weeks to prepare the samples for the *collection* depending on how many models or samples are to be included. The designer, pattern cutter and sample machinist produce the samples from the sample lengths of cloth that the designer selected earlier in the season. From the sample collection there will be many items that do not work either technically or from a design point of view – they may not fit in with the final overall theme of the collection, or by the time they are produced look out of date or just be a *beast* (an item that simply does not work). Most design houses estimate at least 20% wastage at this stage.

Factors in the growth of the ready-to-wear industry

The advent of immense department *stores* in the mid 19th century which became the emporiums of luxury goods on a scale never before envisaged was a huge boost to the growth of the wholesale dress industry. A seemingly limitless variety of items and a vast selection of types of clothing could all be seen in one place, compared, tried on and bought on credit (see Chapter 9).

Cloth manufacturers and garment producers have always by necessity worked hand-in-glove.

Without cloth, garments cannot be produced and without garment production, cloth cannot be sold in the huge quantities that keep this industry going – the soft furnishing industry uses cloth but in nothing like the quantities and varieties used by the garment industry.

The textile industry mechanised its production nearly a hundred years before the garment industry. This is partly because textiles are a flat commodity and clothing is three-dimensional and therefore more complex, and partly because of the inventions that transformed the textile industry overnight. The crafts of spinning, weaving, dyeing and printing that made up the sequence of processes that produce cloth were revolutionised by inventors such as James Hargreaves and Richard Arkwright in the 1760s.

The regulating or supporting bodies

France

Ready-to-wear has its own set of bodies and associations to ensure its standards are maintained, just like couture. In France, under the auspices of the Fédération Française de la Couture, du Prêt-à-Porter des Couturiers et des Créateurs de Mode, the Chambre Syndicale de la Couture Parisienne, founded in 1868, is responsible for couture whilst its sister body the Chambre Syndicale du Prêt-à-Porter des Couturiers et Créateurs de Mode, set up in 1973, is responsible for ready-to-wear. At first, couturiers merely simplified their couture models for a less expensive market. In 1960, eleven couturiers formed a group showing prêt-à-porter collections two weeks before their couture collections. The eleven were Carven, Claude Rivière, Grès-Speciale, Guy Laroche, Jacques Griffe-Evolution, Jacques Heim-Vedette, Jean Dessès-Diffusion, Lanvin-Castillo, Madeleine de Rauche, Maggy Rouff-Extension and Nina Ricci. This group later became known as the Association des Maisons Françaises de Couture-en-Gros which by 1962 had twenty-one wholesale members. The Fédération Française de la Couture, du Prêt-à-Porter et des Créateurs de Mode was formed in 1973 to include the ready-to-wear designers who then became known as the Créateurs. At the same time the Chambre Syndicale de la Mode Masculine was formed for ready-to-wear menswear designers (see Appendix II).

Britain

In Britain, the Model House Group was formed in 1947 by fourteen London fashion wholesalers. During the 1950s it was reorganised into an association of twenty-seven manufacturers with the name The Fashion House Group of London whose members included Aquascutum, Brenner, Deréta, Frank Usher, Amies Ready-to-Wear, Linzi, Polly Peck, Rembrandt, Spectator Sports, Susan Small and Vernervogue. This organisation later became the London Designer Collections, run by Annette Worsley-Taylor, and included Bellville Sassoon, Wendy Dagworthy, Shelagh Brown, Betty Jackson and Jasper Conran amongst others. Its successor, now known as the British Fashion Council (BFC), was set up in the early 1980s to promote British design worldwide. The BFC organises London Fashion Week and the annual British Fashion Awards and comes under the overall control of the British Apparel and Textile Confederation, BATC (see Appendix I).

Italy

The Camera Nazionale della Moda Italiana, founded in 1958, supports, promotes and helps organise Italian fashion as a whole. It was through the prompting of the haute couture Camera Nazionale dell'Alta Moda (started in 1951 by Giovani Battista Giorgini) that this organisation was formed. It aims to coordinate the individual fashion companies, liaise with the press and organise a fashion calendar (see Appendix III).

America

The Fashion Group International (FGI), which in many ways is the American equivalent of the Chambre Syndicale, is slightly different as it deals primarily with ready-to-wear. It was set up in 1928 at the instigation of Edna Woolman Chase, editor-in-chief of *American Vogue*, with seventeen influential fashion businesswomen including Elizabeth Arden, Eleanor Roosevelt, Helena Rubenstein, Carmel Snow and Claire McCardell. Their aims were, and still are, straightforward: the advancement of professionalism in fashion, the provision of a public forum for contemporary fashion issues, the presentation of fashion trends, the recognition of businesswomen's achievements, the promotion of career opportunities, the provision of an inter-fashion networking system and the administration of the FGI Foundation. This Foundation was set up to promote fashion education, provide scholarships and career counselling, and sponsor educational seminars.

Another American body with a similar function is the Council of Fashion Designers of America (CFDA), which is a non-profit-making trade association whose membership consists of 258 of America's foremost fashion and accessory designers. It was founded in 1962 to 'further the position of fashion design as a recognised branch of American art and culture'. Its founding members include Bill Blass, Donald Brooks, Rudi Gernreich, Norman Norell, Arnold Scaasi, Adele Simpson and Pauline Trigère. The CFDA sponsors fashion scholarships and has a huge charity commitment. It helps to organise New York fashion week (see Appendix IV).

Ready-to-wear versus haute couture

The snobbery of the haute couture establishment from the beginning of the 20th century until the 1960s is, today, difficult to understand. The ready-to-wear market and its producers were considered to be of quite another order.

Well-dressed women of 'high society' went only to their couturier, choosing models from a collection, ordering items with the help of the vendeuse, being fitted – going through the complicated routine that, probably, their mothers had gone through before them. They may have bought boutique clothes off-the-peg but only from their couturier and even then these had to be altered by the fitter to couture standards. Smart women without these pretensions or habits would buy wholesale clothes from exclusive department stores, such as Harrods or Marshall and Snelgrove in London, Kendal Milne in Manchester or Jenners in Edinburgh. Labels such as Frederick Starke, Deréta, Susan Small, Dorville and Frank Usher were producing high quality garments that were usually inspired by the Paris couturiers but not truly original designs. This was the main criticism levelled at the ready-to-wear manufacturers by the guardian bodies of haute couture. As mentioned earlier, Frederick Starke was firmly rebuffed by the Incorporated Society of London Fashion Designers when he sought a liaison between the London Model House Group and the Society. Even couture designers such as Bunny Rogers at Fortnum and Mason or Mark Luker at Jay's were not considered of the highest order because they were based in a department store. However exclusive Fortnum and Mason was to the woman in the street, for the couture snob it could not be compared with visiting one's couturier in an exclusive house in Mayfair. There was, of course, also a difference in quality: however good the quality of the ready-to-wear garments, they were mass-produced and lacked the impeccable hand finishes that were the hallmark of a couture garment.

The Japanese influence

The first sign that Japan might have a place on the world fashion stage was when Kansai Yamamoto opened an avant-garde shop in London's Fulham Road. In the early 1970s, using traditional kimono techniques, oversized obis and brilliant colour combinations, his sensational clothes were famously photographed on the six-foot German model, Veruschka, by Richard Avedon. This was the height of the *ethnic* movement and Yamamoto's look was completely appropriate. Again in London, Kenzo designed a range of innovative and seminal knitwear and, later, opened his flagship shop, Jap, in Place des Victoires in Paris. Issey Miyake trained in Paris at the Chambre Syndicale School and was assistant designer to Guy Laroche and Givenchy in the mid 1960s. His early work gave little hint of what he is so famous for today, experimental structural shapes and innovative fabric manipulation, because then, although high fashion, his clothes were in the tradition of good French prêt-à-porter. The other Japanese designers who had a huge impact on Paris ready-to-wear were Rei Kawakubo and Yohji Yamamato. On the scene in 1969 was Kawakubo whose first and spectacular collection was taken up by *Elle*. The collection had what the French call a *garçonne* or boyish look, and when asked by the *Elle* journalists what it was about, she said 'comme des garçons' – like the boys – and the world famous label, Comme des Garçons, was born. Her work started a trend in 'non-cutting' cutting which, together with her compatriot and friend Yohji Yamamoto, changed for almost a decade the whole concept of cutting and *construction* of high-fashion clothing.

All these designers now operate from Paris and Tokyo and it is probably Yohji Yamamoto who has the strongest influence on current fashion. A look that was sombre, stark and apparently difficult has somehow, through the osmosis of the fashion process, become highly saleable.

The emergence of Belgium

By the early 1990s a new fashion force was emerging from Belgium. The Flanders School of Fashion in Antwerp was producing designers of world class: Ann Demeulemeester, Dirk

Bikkembergs, Martin Margiela and Dries Van Noten. These designers produced looks like 'deconstruct' and 'rock-tailoring' that influenced fashion for the next decade. The 'Antwerp Six' first showed in London in 1986. Several of these designers, including Ann Demeulemeester, have opened premises in Paris, and Dries Van Noten, still with a base in Antwerp, has showrooms in both Paris and Milan and is an associate member of France's illustrious Fédération. Belgium is now well established as a fashion force through the work of these designers.

Italy's role in ready-to-wear

Italy's fashion history is very different. Together with its great couturiers it has always had a reputation for high quality boutiques selling luxury items, such as scarves, accessories, jewellery or items like the famous Pucci beach pyjamas and sportswear.

Even in 1951, when Giorgini launched the Italian couturiers on to the world stage, he had an eye on the American wholesale market. The buyers of department stores like Marshall Field, I. Magnin, B. Altman and Bergdorf Goodman were guests at that first showing in Florence. By the mid 1960s, Italy had established a flourishing and enviable ready-to-wear base.

Companies such as Basile, Cadette, Genny, Maxmara and Complice not only employed home-grown talent, for example Gianni Versace at Callaghan and Genny, Giorgio Armani at Erreuno and Moschino at Cadette, but also had the foresight to employ French designers, including Claude Montana at Complice, Anne-Marie Beretta at Maxmara and Karl Lagerfeld at Fendi, and English designers such as Keith Varty and Allan Cleaver at Byblos.

Italy today exerts a huge influence on the world fashion market – Prada, Gucci, Armani and Moschino are household names, and Missoni, Gigli and Marnie still influence high street copies. Milan's twice-yearly designer shows now rival those in Paris. Miuccia Prada, designer and proprietor of the huge but still privately owned fashion empire, is the envy of many an American fashion giant. A similar company with a similar background is Gucci, but its upturn in fortune in 1994 was due to employing designer Tom Ford as creative director and, more recently (in 2001) the acquisition of Alexander McQueen and Stella McCartney. Giorgio Armani's steady but undeniable hold on stylish dressing is entirely due to his own talent and philosophy.

British ready-to-wear

The list of British ready-to-wear designers has lengthened since their first impact in the 1960s. Betty Jackson, Nicole Farhi, Jasper Conran, Joseph Ettedgui and Katherine Hamnett are part of the fashion scene in Britain, but Rifat Ozbek, Pearce Fionda and Hussein Chalayan, not to mention Galliano and McQueen, have found it difficult to survive the vagaries of the British fashion industry if not taken up by a multinational company. Britain has the talent but not necessarily the backing.

America: the first in ready-to-wear

America may find it difficult to name many couturiers among its designers, but in ready-to-wear it is prolific and sophisticated. Its huge mass production output, plus a history in marketing strategy that is second to none, give it the edge in this field. Good ready-to-wear designers were prevalent in America long before any emerged in Europe; for example Hattie Carnegie was operating in New York as early as 1918. It was Carnegie who spawned Norman Norell, Jean Louis (the film designer) and the inimitable Claire McCardell. The easy sportswear look exemplified by McCardell was also the forte of Bonnie Cashin and, in another way, of Bill Blass and Geoffrey Beene. This look, later taken up by Norma Kamali, Mary McFadden and Halston, is evident today in the work of Ralph Lauren, Calvin Klein and Donna Karan.

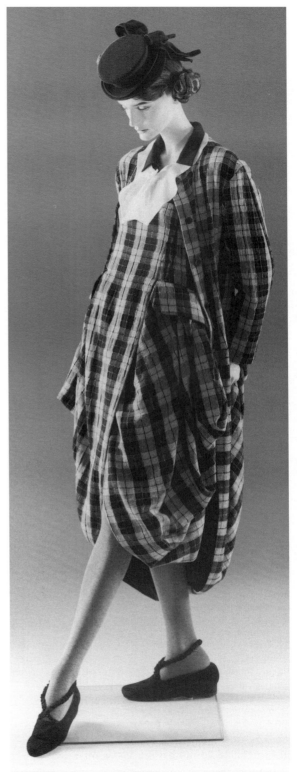

Above: Jean-Paul Gaultier's play on blue denim – a chic button-through dress of 1988.

Right: Before he took up his appointment at Christian Dior, John Galliano produced his own collection under his own name in London; this masterly coat-dress is a 1987 example with felt hat and shoes by Patrick Cox.

A 1986 example of the great Italian designer Giorgio Armani's impeccable suit cutting for women.

A sleeveless shift with patriotic intarsia panel by the American designer Ralph Lauren, dated 1991.

From Dries Van Noten's spring/summer show held in the Ecole Nationale Supérieure des Beaux-Arts in Paris, October 2002.

An outfit from the Dries Van Noten's spring/summer collection.

Another outfit from Dries Van Noten's spring/summer collection.

Chapter 3
Mass Production

The mass production process – Production – Sizing – Design strategies in mass production – Lines within a design house – Offshore production – Ethical trading – New trends

The mass production process

The clothing industry is as mechanised as any in the industrialised world and the number of workers that it employs compares with giants such as the motor and other product manufacturing industries. The route from design to finished garment is complicated and in many ways mimics the processes that the original dressmaker or tailor used in the past. These processes have been broken down into a sequence: the pattern, the sizing, the lay plan, the cutting out, the sewing together and the finishing.

Before the pattern is made the fabric is tested for abrasion, pillage, shrinkage and so on. The *pattern* has to ensure that not only the desired silhouette, details, fit, hang and fall match the designer's sketch but also that built into this pattern are instructions on how the garment is to be assembled. This is achieved by a series of coded marks that denote the width and form of the seam allowances, notches to indicate where the seams are to be, drill holes to show darts and pocket placing. The correct *sizing* is achieved by a process called *grading* which is a technique that uses the master pattern (usually size 12 in UK sizing) to develop a series of increasing or decreasing sizes for each design which can be anything from size 8 to 22 and even higher. Nowadays grading is usually done by computer and relies on complicated mathematical calculations. The introduction of computer-aided grading has speeded up this process ten-fold, but the computer is only a tool, it is the *grader* who is the irreplaceable expert in the grading process.

The next stage is the *lay plan* which is a method of placing pattern pieces on to the cloth economically, not unlike a jigsaw puzzle. This placing is affected by the particular characteristics of the fabric: *grain lines*, checks and stripes, *pile* or *one-way fabrics*. The *cutting out* is either manual or automated. If manual, the cloth is *laid up* either by two people (one person controlling the straight edge of the fabric) or by one person operating a *cloth-lay spreading machine*. The cloth is laid up in layers with tissue paper or its equivalent between each roll of fabric to distinguish dye batch and colour variation. A minimum of 5 layers to a maximum of 100 can be laid up in this way, depending on the thickness of the cloth and accuracy required. A manual lay is cut using either a *band knife* or a *straight knife*.

Multi-layered automated cutting is now carried out on a specially designed vacuum-compressed table where 25 layers can be laid and cut at once. The cutting is done with a mechanical band knife and is now mostly computer-aided and entirely automatic. The cut pieces are *bundled* together and *docketed*.

Assembly is where the garment is sewn together. This assembly is itself broken down into component parts; the collar, pockets, sleeves and cuffs for example will be assembled separately and then attached to the garment body or *shell* which will itself have been assembled

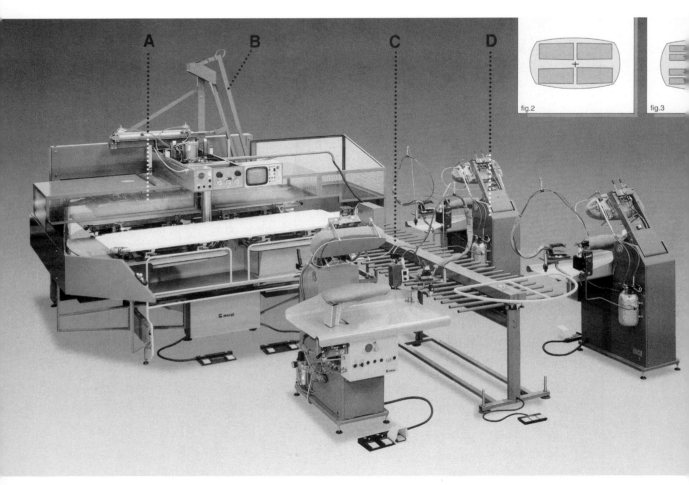

A highly sophisticated industrial trouser press from the company Macpi.

Two views of a modern garment factory floor with computer-aided cutting tables and cutting heads in use. Only one skilled operative is required to oversee several machines at once.

separately in advance. Each of these processes is carried out by a different operative who works on a mechanised assembly line, now usually also computer-aided so that, for example, the collar is dropped off at the machinist with the most collar expertise, the overlocking at the overlocker and so on. Each design will have a different assembly plan worked out in advance on the prototype which will usually have been assembled by one expert sample machinist with the help of a garment technologist.

The *finishing*, until a short time ago done by hand, is now mechanised, with the technical innovations in **blind hemmers** superseding the hand finishers. In some manufacturing companies, pressing takes place during assembly and is called 'under pressing', but the usual practice is to use one of the sophisticated pressing units to press the finished garment and possibly to blow hot air through it. This is then passed by the quality controller and packed ready for distribution.

Production

There are many ways in which manufacturing companies or **production units** can operate. They can be integral with the parent design company or they can be entirely separate entities, such as **outwork factories** that are contracted by the design company to deal with production only (that is the manufacturing of the garment from **production pattern** to finished garment).

There has been a policy over the past few years to move more and more into outwork factory production. This is probably due to the introduction of CAD/CAM, computer-aided design and computer-aided manufacture. These systems are very expensive and are efficient at dealing with a huge throughput of garments, which many of the smaller design manufacturers cannot afford. Often these outwork production factories started as design manufacturing companies who found they could handle a much

larger production capacity than their own design company warranted and, in order to repay their capital outlay on new computer-aided plant, they took on extra work. Where giant companies like Marks and Spencer used this production capability, many design manufacturing companies went over to solely working as outworkers and gave up their own design manufacturing. They were able to upgrade their production, increase their turnover and improve their time and motion, through sophisticated **just-in-time technology**, to the point where they lost interest in their design production capabilities and consequently simply remain profitable outwork units working for others.

The outwork factory can be anywhere in the world. In the early 1970s many companies found that they could get quality production at a competitive price in Hong Kong. After this initial foray into the Far East the production market widened to include Taiwan, Thailand, Singapore and later the whole Pacific Rim. Now China, India, Sri Lanka, Turkey and Mauritius can all produce garments at a lower price than Continental Europe, and even eastern European countries and the Baltic States are being exploited because of their cheap labour. Many of the Far East companies were quick to invest in computer-aided manufacturing systems and therefore were in many ways a better option than domestic factories. Agents acting for these manufacturing units are approaching well-known design companies offering garment manufacture throughout the world and have many factories on their books. This in itself presents another problem, quality control, which in turn has produced a new professional, the roving QC (quality controller) whose job it is to travel from factory to factory checking standards.

Manufacturing plants of course vary in size, productivity and innovation, but many factories have cutting rooms the size of football pitches. These huge areas are designed so that the bolts of cloth can be delivered by the hauliers' lorries at one end, straight on to the cutting tables, be

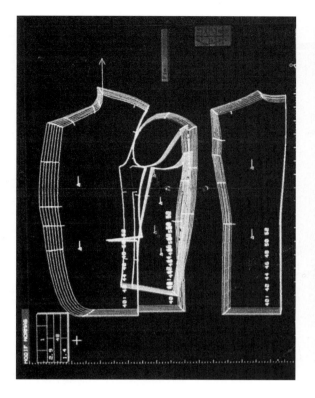

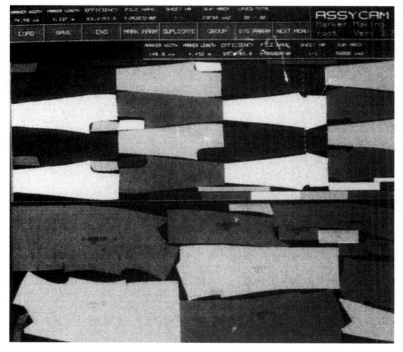

Top left: a graded pattern jacket nest.

Top right: a jacket pattern. (From Gerber Technology.)

Left: a lay plan.

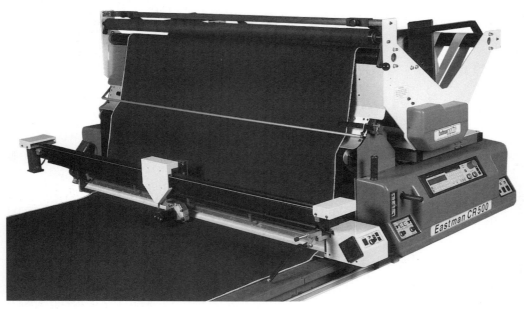

A laying up machine, which spreads the fabric on to the table. (From Eastman.)

A fully automated computer-aided cutting table with cutting head in place. (From Gerber Technology.)

An operative using a band knife.

A computer-aided cutting head.
(From Gerber Technology.)

A cutting tool. (From Eastman.)

Marking tools. (From Eastman.)

cut, distributed to operatives, machined together and subsequently delivered to the retail outlet or contracting fashion companies within a matter of hours. Ideally, the whole operation from cloth delivery to distribution of garments should fit in with the now popular concept of just-in-time technology thus avoiding costly storage costs.

Vertical companies are those doing their own design, manufacture and distribution, which includes retail trading, a particularly British phenomenon. Marks and Spencer is a good example. The large design and production companies were for a time considered a dying breed; however, the need to shorten lead times has led to changes in this area where some companies like the Spanish firm Zara have reverted to the practice of operating everything under one roof (see Chapter 9).

Sizing

Sizing constitutes one of the major obstacles to manufacturing multiple garments, the primary function of mass production. Human beings vary so much in size – height, girth and shape – that the only real method of ensuring a perfect fit is made-to-measure clothing, but for the ready-to-wear and mass production industries this is, quite obviously, not an option. Universal sizing systems have taxed the minds of dressmakers and tailors over the centuries and many different formulas have been invented, tested and implemented. Common measuring systems and formulas, now part of everyday life, were for a long period arbitrary and personal to the particular tailor or dressmaker using them. Even the ubiquitous tape measure was not introduced until about 1800. In the past, most garments were constructed by taking an earlier garment apart and copying it. Universal sizing systems have always been the ideal, but many factors come into play when deciding on the perfect formula. The typical Anglo-Saxon woman's figure is very different from that of her Latin counterpart; the Japanese and the Afro-Caribbean figure

may nominally be the same size but they have very different shapes. European, American and British sizing systems are all different. Manufacturers want to flatter their customers and consequently many call their size 12 a size 10. In order to overcome some of these difficulties, a worldwide sizing survey was recently instigated. The British contingent, called Size UK, was organised by University College London and the Department of Trade and Industry. It measured over ten thousand men and women in the UK.

Design strategies in mass production

To giants like Levi, Gap, Matalan and Marks and Spencer, design has become the science of delivering the item the public is 'just about to want'. This needs very careful research, planning, prediction and advertising. Teams of designers, researchers, fabrication and textile innovators scour the world for ideas, trends, fabrics, colour and texture data. These teams will then make a visual presentation to the directors and the marketing experts, usually in the form of a *mood board* or a video presentation, showing their research and possible design suggestions and predictions. The greatest buying power is with the young, and many companies include music trends in their prediction thinking. The forecasting companies such as Worth Global Style Network (WGSN) can supply seasonal, monthly and even weekly information on what is happening at different levels – on the streets, in the capitals of the world, in celebrity society or high fashion.

Lines within a design house

Whereas, in the past, a couture house had a boutique line and perhaps a wholesale range – a watered down, cheaper version of its couture collection – now the designer houses can have many different *lines* with different levels of quality, price, market and production. With a company that runs several fashion lines on several

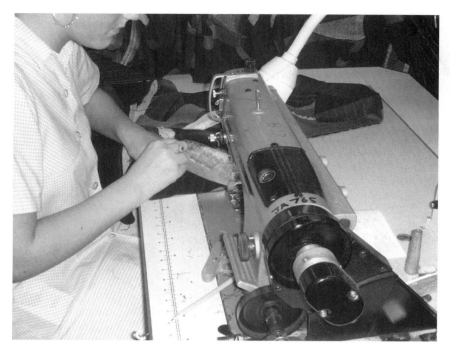

Skilled machinist at work.

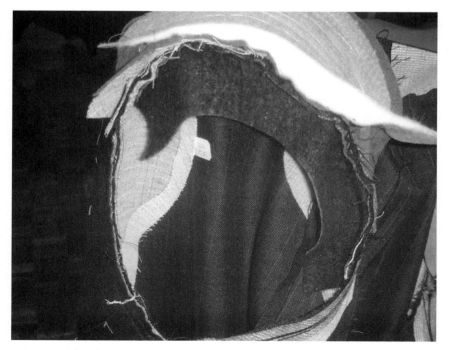

Using specialised machinery to manipulate a sleeve head.

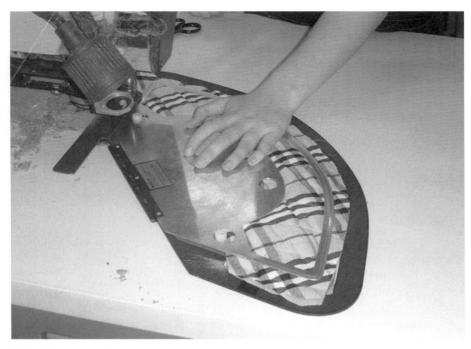

Collar jig or template.

Completed collar.

levels, for example Donna Karan, DKNY and Donna Karan Jeans, the quality, pricing and location of production will vary. Rip-offs have no traceable roots, and since so many are illegal, undercover operations and research into this area is difficult if not impossible. At last, high street companies are employing well-known designers to design commercial ranges, for example Jasper Conran, Pearce Fionda and John Rocha at Debenhams.

Offshore production

Competition for work between the different outwork production companies is very great, and solving the equation for quality, consistency, cheapness and prompt and reliable supply is paramount for both the contractor, design company and the contracted production supplier.

A few years ago, the Pacific Rim, the Indian subcontinent and eastern Europe relied on very cheap labour, out-of-date machinery and factories with terrible working conditions. Now, however, these countries have invested in the latest equipment, and modern factories with computer-aided manufacture and technology are commonplace. As this becomes more sophisticated and as more processes become computerised, the outlay has to be justified by bulk orders in millions of items instead of thousands. Although many larger British companies have gone offshore to find cheaper production, smaller companies cannot afford nor do they have sufficient *volume* to do this and therefore still use home production, usually in the form of outwork factory companies. Britain's fashion industry, including its garment manufacturing capability, has fallen from being the country's third biggest industry to its seventh.

Smaller companies of the level of Monsoon and Oasis who cannot afford to experiment can often 'go on the back' of the huge companies like

An Eton conveyer system distributing cut parts to the appropriate operative.

Marks and Spencer, because the groundwork, including ethical trading, will already have been done.

Ethical trading

The question of cheap labour is a moot point. The employment of children, women and certainly young male teenagers is glossed over by the hungry garment industry. Assurances that their methods are always ethical are open to question. The irony of the situation is that the public who demand cheaper items, who even see this very cheapness as a moral right, is the real exploiter of cheap and child labour. Very expensive items made in a Parisian atelier are expensive because the expert labour is properly paid.

Because of outside pressure from agencies concerned with the welfare of young and exploited labour, ethical considerations have become an issue with garment manufacturers *sourcing* outworkers in the developing world. Many companies have set up units expressly to deal with these considerations. Sourcing new mass production outwork units in different parts of the world is now a major priority with many large fashion companies. New roles have been created to address these priorities and make sure that when setting up overseas outwork factories, ethical targets are met. Child labour is a much more complicated issue than it appears to well-heeled western consumers. Work, however exploitative for a child in a developing country, can mean the difference between life and death, and can offer an alternative to a life of prostitution. Any 'ethical' programme has to have an intimate knowledge of local culture and any judgements must be made in the light of the parameters of this culture.

New trends

The current buzzword in manufacture is mass customisation. This ostensibly is a mass production equivalent of made-to-measure, giving customers the garments that not only exactly fit their body measurements but also fit their particular colour, shape and detailing requirements. Experiments in digital body scanning have led to companies such as the German firm Human Solutions offering such a system. This process may sound over optimistic by present-day standards as it does not yet explain how the complexities of mass production procedures are overcome. It may be some time before this concept hits the high street.

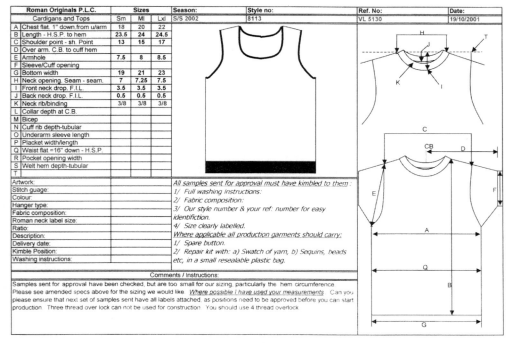

Instruction docket.

Chapter 4
Tailoring

History – Male-dominated craft – Bespoke tailoring – Savile Row –
The supremacy of the English tailors – Royal patronage and influence – The ethos
of English tailoring – Specialist tailors –Tailoring techniques – The bespoke
tailoring process – Tailoring cloth suppliers – Couture tailoring

History

Tailoring, traditionally a male-dominated trade, has its roots in the medieval trade guilds. Thought by some to have originated as the undergarments for armour – constructed with padding and particular pattern shapes to prevent chaffing and make the wearing of armour more comfortable – tailoring has certainly always had close associations with military dress. Many of the items now regarded as *classics* in menswear were first of all designed for particular military functions – the greatcoat, the trench coat, the flying jacket and the bomber jacket. Several of the London Savile Row tailors, usually considered by the world as the greatest masters of this art, were originally military tailors. The other great tailors were the Jews; for people who were constantly having to move from place to place out of political necessity, tailoring was the ideal trade because it required no permanent premises and could be operated by one person squatting on a bench or even the floor with a needle as his principal tool.

Costume designer David Walker and costume historian Norah Waugh believe that real tailoring did not start until the end of the eighteenth or beginning of the nineteenth century. After studying and taking apart many period items, they have come to the conclusion that, before that time, men's clothes had a distinctly dressmaker quality. A suit made in Germany for the king of Sweden at the end of the 18th century had a quality of make that set it apart from contemporary English items. Royalty of this period still had most of their clothes made in Paris because the tradition of making there was so much better. Not until the strictures put upon tailors in the late 18th century by Beau Brummell, that denizen of taste and perfection of make, did the English tailors' reputation for excellence and style emerge.

Male-dominated craft

The tradition of the male-domination in this craft or industry was not a natural evolution but a distinction enforced by law. Prior to the 18th century it was a punishable offence for a woman to practise tailoring: one daughter of a Hawick tailor was sent to prison for working as her father's *journeyman* (Sanderson, 2001).

Bespoke tailoring

Bespoke means made to order: choosing a style, being measured for this, fitted and taking final delivery of a suit that is individually made and tailored for that customer – a method that is not dissimilar to couture but mostly applies to menswear. In rare cases a woman has a suit made by a man's tailor, but the only real tradition for this is in riding habits. The woman's tailor can be found in the couture house and plays

A 17th century illustration of the tailor haberdasher's craft.

The early 17th century ruff or pickadil as it was called, the speciality of Robert Baker, tailor and the founder of Piccadilly.

a different role, usually as head of the tailoring workroom where the coats and suits are made. Bespoke tailoring has different methods of pattern cutting from couture tailoring; the pattern is usually drafted by the tailor directly on to the cloth in tailor's chalk using yard rules, set squares and, in some cases, French curves, although traditional tailors pride themselves on their ability to draft curves freehand. This drafting is a highly specialised art and calls on drawing skills, mathematical precision and great knowledge.

Savile Row

Savile Row, synonymous throughout the world with the highest level of men's tailoring, is a small street in London's Mayfair. Mayfair, itself always associated with luxury goods, ironically owes its development to a tailor, Robert Baker, a Somerset man, who came to London in the 1590s to make his fortune. He did exactly that by becoming a specialist, as so many tailors did. His specialism was, if not the invention, at least the perfection of the ruff or pickadil as it was then called – the pleated collar that was such a feature of late Elizabethan and early Jacobean fashionable dress. Baker became a clever land speculator and bought several acres of what is

now the area from Pall Mall to Oxford Street including Piccadilly, Haymarket and Golden Square. The mansion he built in Windmill Street was jokingly called Pickadilly Hall after the item of dress that had helped him acquire his wealth. London's Piccadilly is of course named after this.

The next great developer was a rich aristocrat, Richard Boyle, Earl of Burlington, who bought Ten Acre Close, the area behind his mansion, Burlington House, in Piccadilly. His grandson the third Earl, great patron of artists and architects, rebuilt Burlington House and started to build Old Burlington Street, Cork Street, Clifford Street and Boyle Street – names today associated with the world of luxury merchandise. The third Earl married Lady Dorothy Savile and in 1730 built Savile Row and New Burlington Street. These streets were at first inhabited by fashionable noblemen, gentry, actors and celebrities, and 'many gentlewomen', but by the end of the 18th century the more exclusive tradesmen were acquiring premises there.

The term 'Savile Row tailors' applied not only to those in the Row but also to those in the immediate vicinity, Cork Street, Old and New Burlington Streets, Sackville Street, Conduit Street and Clifford Street, in fact all those streets developed by Lord Burlington behind Burlington House.

A contemporary map of the area around Savile Row.

An early print of Burlington House, Piccadilly, the home of London bespoke tailoring

The supremacy of the English tailors

The recognised supremacy of English tailoring can be attributed in part to the Anglomania – a love for all things English – that spread throughout Europe from around 1770 until well into the first half of the next century. The Age of Enlightenment, progress in science and industry and a democratic parliamentary system with a constitutional monarch and a reputation for free speech made England the envy of the world. The style that went with it, non-formal, throwaway, nonchalant and sporty, led to a style of dress that was copied by all those who considered themselves leaders of fashion. Even Marie-Antoinette, the ill-fated queen of France, fell for its charms: for her it meant the shepherdess look, the mock farm at Versailles, and the casual 'undress' seen in Gainsborough portraits. For men it meant fox hunting, thoroughbred horses, fast gigs, gambling and the clothes that went with this lifestyle – riding jackets, riding breeches, riding boots

and hard hats that would stay on in a strong wind. It also meant hardwearing woollen broadcloth for coats, doe skin pants (pantaloons) and white linen shirts. This was the look and style epitomised by Beau Brummell.

Royal patronage and influence

In the late 19th and early 20th centuries, Edward VII and his grandson Edward VIII, later the Duke of Windsor, not only were very fashionable but also between them invented, or at least introduced, many items or ways of wearing clothes that have become part of the everyday vocabulary of menswear tailoring. The Duke of Windsor wrote in *Windsor Revisited*,

My grandfather unquestionably had a wider influence on masculine fashions than any member of the Royal Family since George IV. He was a good friend to the tailors of Savile Row, consolidating the position of London as the international sartorial shrine for men, as already Paris was for women. When he visited Marienbad, as he got into the habit of doing each year incognito as the Duke of Lancaster to 'take the waters', tailors from Paris, Vienna and all parts of the Continent used to gather and follow him around surreptitiously photographing him and jotting down notes on his clothes.

He went on to quote Prince von Bulow on Edward VII: 'the uncontested *arbiter elegantiarium*', adding, 'in the country in which unquestionably the gentlemen dressed best, he was the best-dressed gentleman. Few since George IV and his friend Brummell have worn civilian clothes better.'

The ethos of English tailoring

The worldwide reputation of English tailoring depends on an ethos introduced by Beau Brummell and disseminated by the masters of the craft in Savile Row. Beau Brummell or George Bryan Brummell (1778–1840) was the son of Lord North's private secretary and reputedly the grandson of a valet. A caustic sense of humour and an elegant and languid manner caught the eye of the Prince of Wales even while he was still at Eton and for a time the pair became inseparable. His influence on the Prince and on fashionable London society became immense and his immaculate dress sense was a turning point in men's style. The rigours that he imposed upon the English gentleman's dressing habits set the seal of the supremacy of English tailoring and the method whereby styles evolved depending on individual habits and taste and is a tribute to the rapport between the Englishman and his tailor, which still holds good today. This rigour was a rigour of subtlety laced with a certain English eccentricity, which is the hallmark of English not to say British men's fashion.

His rules included 'cloth' (woollen fabric) instead of silk, velvet or brocade, perfectly laundered linen, straight narrow trousers instead of

Anglomania – the typical dress of the English 'milord' which gave rise to the fashion at the end of the 18th century for all things English in male dressing.

Beau Brummell, the inspiration for the inimitable style that was English tailoring.

The Count d'Orsay who, after Brummell's retirement to France, became the leader of men's fashion in London.

satin knee breeches, and riding boots instead of high-heeled shoes; plain simple country dressing but of a sensational quality and style and the highest order of cleanliness and grooming.

Brummell's own tailors were Schweitzer and Davidson in Cork Street, Weston in Old Bond Street and Meyer in Conduit Street. Both Schweitzer and Meyer also worked for the Prince of Wales. Meyer, founded by the German John Meyer, exists today as Meyer and Mortimer specialising in military tailoring as part of Jones, Chalk and Davidson at 6 Sackville Street, a company still frequented by aristocratic Scots clients – the original Mortimer was an Edinburgh gunsmith.

Brummell was succeeded in his role as arbiter of sartorial taste first by Lord Alvenly and then by the Count d'Orsay who was a six foot three French aristocrat and the lover of the notorious Lady Blessington. D'Orsay's tailor was Henry Creed, grandson of James Creed who came to London in 1710 from Leicestershire to become a tailor and found a dynasty of tailors, and grandfather of Charles Creed, the London couturier of the 1950s and 1960s. Charles Creed in his book on the family, *Maid to Measure*, says, 'D'Orsay wore clothes splendidly, he knew everybody that was anybody and whither he went the beaumonde followed' (Creed, 1961). Henry Creed was established at 33 Conduit Street, two doors away from Meyer and Mortimer. Count d'Orsay adopted England and English taste as so many Frenchmen of this period did – as late as 1836 the Parisian *Journal des Tailleurs* was promoting the idea, 'In the near future we will have achieved the level of perfection generally attributed to the English'.

Specialist tailors

Specialism has been the spur for the founding of many of the great British tailoring houses. Gieves and Hawkes, the naval tailors, started supplying the uniforms for Nelson and his fellow officers in the Napoleonic Wars. With their first premises in Portsmouth, the home of the British Navy, they were able to take advantage of the fact that Great Britain was the first country to introduce a naval uniform for ship's companies of men-o'-war. Uniform, that 'distinctive dress of uniform material, colour and cut, worn by a particular military, naval or other force' (as defined in the *Shorter Oxford English Dictionary*), was not only a method of distinguishing a particular service or regiment, but also a great leveller. At the same time it meant that tailors had a captive clientele as members of each force had to provide their own uniforms as part of the force's regulations. Many companies set up in the appropriate town, as Gieves and Hawkes did with their first shop in Portsmouth; they also set up the clever merchandising ploy of kitting out naval cadets as they entered naval college, thus ensuring lifelong clients for their company.

Aldershot, the British Army headquarters, had about twenty tailors in the town at the beginning of the 20th century. Today only Glover and Ryding caters for military clients. This company, set up in World War I by Mr Glover, is still the official tailor to the King's Own Scottish Borderers, supplying not only the uniform but also the appropriate kilt, trews and tam-o'-shanter. The late Mr Ryding, the father of the present proprietor Donald Ryding, was the expert on cutting trews, the tartan trousers that are so much a part of the distinctive Scottish uniform. This is an art in itself; in order to properly match the checks, the trouser hem is the starting point so that a regiment standing in line will all have the same check at foot level and hence appear much more uniform whatever the height of the soldier. Another quirk of trews is that they have no side seam. Paper patterns are drafted individually for Glover and Ryding's clients; only where the customer is a stock size will a standard block pattern be used and adapted to individual measurements.

Of the great Savile Row tailors, probably the oldest is Adeney and Boutroy who can trace their roots back to the City of London in 1704.

Ron Pescod, the nonagenarian present proprietor, took over the business from his father who specialised in clerical tailoring for archbishops, bishops and, presumably, very well-dressed clergymen. They moved into Savile Row in the mid 18th century and were therefore the first tailors to establish themselves in the street that has since, throughout the world, become the byword for excellence in tailoring and men's clothing. Huntsman, Henry Poole, Gieves and Hawkes and Kilgour, French and Standbury are all prime examples of this tradition and were established if not in the 18th century at least by the early 19th century. Savile Row also allowed the 'trendier' tailors to establish themselves in the street or nearby – Blades, Tommy Nutter and Mr Fish were the tailoring equivalent of Mary Quant, André Courrèges and Ossie Clark in the 1960s. As part of the new breed of Savile Row tailors, Ozwald Boateng confusingly calls his ready-to-wear collections Bespoke Couture at 9 Vigo, whilst his new bespoke premises are at 12a Savile Row.

Tailoring techniques

The whole essence of tailoring is its construction, or 'shaping' as it was known in the past. This construction which makes two-dimensional fabric hold a three-dimensional form on its own, even before being placed on a body, is achieved by cut and a series of underpinnings or interlinings. Through the medium of the tailored jacket the good tailor is able to transform and rebuild his client's figure: broaden the shoulders, straighten the back, diminish the waist and give the impression of a much fuller chest. This is done through the construction of a body made out of layers of canvasses, horsehair, padding and tape – this construction is inserted between the main cloth body of the garment and the lining and is called the *interlining*. These interlinings of different weaves, rigidity, thickness and fabric composition and their use are very much part of the tailor's art. They must hold the garment in the required shape or form but still appear soft and natural. The traditional tailor helps mould the new shape by *pad-stitching*, pressing and shrinking techniques which hold the new shape in place permanently, like a pre-formed body.

The principle of the pre-formed, interlining body shapes as practised by the bespoke tailor has been copied and reinvented by the ready-to-wear and mass production manufacturers. Using modern technological innovations, interlining manufacturers have come up with many different weights, textures and adhesive properties for their products. Without these new types of interlining, the softer suit, so much part of Giorgio Armani's signature, would not have been possible. Specific types of interlining have specific tasks: collar canvas for the collar, horsehair canvas for holding the shoulder and chest areas, red-edged canvas for fronts, pocket canvas and pocket *duck* for pockets, and a softer canvas for hems and cuffs. To prevent stretching, edges can be taped. Different types of shoulder pads can entirely change the silhouette of the jacket and even give the wearer a figure he does not really have. The lining on a classic tailored jacket is made from two different fabrics, one for the sleeve, usually striped, and another for the body of the jacket. This not only helps the jacket to fall properly but also helps it to slip on and off easily.

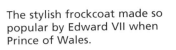

The stylish frockcoat made so popular by Edward VII when Prince of Wales.

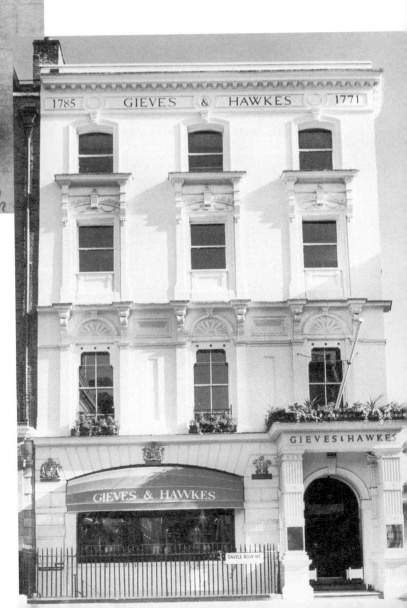

Gieves and Hawkes, originally the naval tailor, occupies this splendid building at No. 1 Savile Row, on the corner of Old Burlington Street, in the heart of the tailoring enclave.

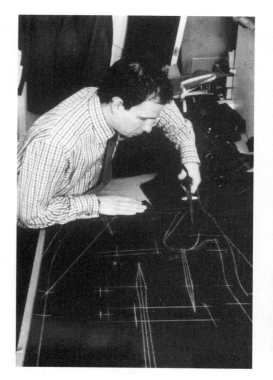

Behind the scenes at Henry Poole. Top left: a cutter. Top right: a tailor. Above: a workroom.

The bespoke tailoring process

The *Oxford English Dictionary* definition of bespoke is 'to engage beforehand, to order goods'. Thus the bespoke tailoring process is initiated by the customer engaging the tailor to make a garment individually for him. The client must then be *measured*. This in itself is quite a complicated undertaking as it is from this complex set of measurements that any drafting or pattern making will be done. These measurements must always be taken in the same place on specific areas of the body – across the chest, the back, the shoulder area and the arm length, the waist and hips, the outside leg and inside leg. These measurements are taken with a tape measure – this, surprisingly, is a relatively new invention. The science of body measurement was a breakthrough and was preceded by a trial and error method involving copying previously used garments. Even the units of inches or centimetres were not universally standardised until the latter part of the 18th century, but 'by 1820 the use of the tape measure by tailors appears to have been quite common' (Aldrich, 2000).

From the measurements the tailor constructs or *drafts* the pattern, either on to paper or card or even sometimes directly on to the cloth. Toîles or calico prototypes, as used in women's couture and ready-to-wear manufacture, are not used in men's tailoring. The pattern is placed on and marked out on the cloth, first in *tailor's chalk* and then with white cotton thread; this is called *tacking* or *basting* and can be done using *tailor tacking* or *trace tacking* to mark the sewing line more permanently. The pattern pieces are then cut out with tailor's shears. Being able to cut deftly, precisely and with verve is a great part of the tailor's art and why of course they were called tailors, from *tailler*, the French for 'to cut'.

The cut pieces are then tacked or sewn together by hand to prepare the garment for the first fitting. This tacking must be very precisely executed otherwise the tacked item will not give an accurate indication of the *fit* and *balance* of the garment. The client will be asked to attend the first fitting and will have to stand for quite a time while the fit is checked, the style modified and the alterations marked with either pins or chalk. The client can at this point make suggestions, but since the cloth is already cut these can only be minor.

After the fitting all the alterations must be carefully noted and indicated. It must be remembered that the tailor who does the fitting will pass the more mundane work on to a tailoring hand who must understand the set of alteration marks made by the fitter or tailor. At this point the preliminary tacking is usually undone and the new alterations marked on the flat. The garment will then be tacked together again for the next fitting. The client will then be booked for a further fitting where parts of the garment may have been already machined together. When the tailor and client are satisfied that the garment is right, then linings, buttons and other trimmings are discussed. The garment will then be taken apart for the final time and the final alterations made. When the tailor is completely satisfied, he or his assistants will machine the garment together. It should be added that the client must be used to this method of making to judge the final appearance from the fitting stages – the garment will not be pressed, the trousers will have no creases and the revers may still have the canvas and horsehair interlings showing.

Tailoring cloth suppliers

The introduction of 'cloth', woollen fabric, in the latter half of the 18th century in fashionable men's tailoring was at first a specifically English phenomenon. Upper-class men had previously favoured silks, satins and brocades for their suits. The rage for unostentatious dress, said to be introduced by Beau Brummell, meant that cloth jackets and breeches and 'country laundered' linen shirts, in Brummell's own words, became high fashion. A strange fact in fashionable menswear has been its tendency to take on

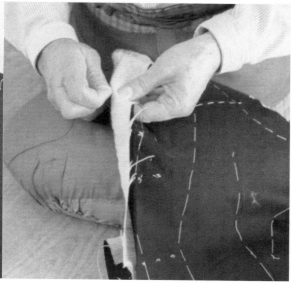

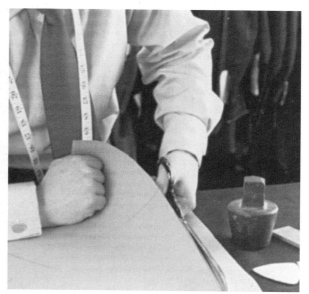

Top left: a suit tacked ready for a fitting at Huntsman.

Top right: a tailor pad-stitching a revers at Huntsman.

Left: The cutter at Huntsman making the card pattern.

the character of the sportswear of the day. Riding clothes of the 18th century became the formal wear of the 19th century, whereas high fashion formal wear of the previous era is relegated to servants. Footmen in the 19th century wore the formal dress of the eighteenth century. The evening tailcoat of the 19th century became the waiter's uniform of the 20th. In France and the rest of Europe, woollen cloth was reserved for the lower classes – it took the French Revolution to persuade Frenchmen to adopt this very English fashion. The seeds of women's tailoring can be seen in the very masculine woollen cloth riding habit worn by upper-class women in the 18th century.

Above: from Huntsman, showing their waisted, longer jacket silhouette in a typical large windowpane check.

Left: from Henry Poole, a chalk-striped double-breasted suit.

British tailoring relied on the manufacture of top quality cloth. The great centres for woollen manufacture in Britain and famed throughout the world were Galashiels, Hawick, Peebles and Selkirk in the Scottish Borders, the Stroud Valley in the west of England, and Bradford, Halifax and Huddersfield in Yorkshire. The names of these cloths are redolent of their end uses: Barathea, Melton and doe-skin for uniforms; thornproof tweed for sporting activities like hunting, shooting and fishing. So many of these mills no longer exist, decimated by a need to rationalise. Famous for producing the cloth for the Pope's robes, names like Strachan and Upton Lovell have been reduced to making billiard table cloth or tennis ball cloth. Prince of Wales check, herringbone, birdseye and chalk stripe are patterns synonymous with British tailoring, now more probably manufactured in Italy or Japan. Worsted woollen from Huddersfield, which Balenciaga called the finest cloth in the world, ceased manufacture to make way for cheaper man-made cloths: a false economy as now the factories have disappeared altogether. Savile Row still boasts several high quality woollen merchants such as Wain Shiell, Holland and Sherry, and Hunt and Winterbotham.

Couture tailoring

Ever since the house of Creed introduced women to men's tailoring in the 1890s, tailoring has been part of the couturier's repertoire. The appropriation of men's tailoring by women began seriously when Henry Creed made his first riding habit for the Duchess of Alba. Gentlemen's tailors had made jackets for women as a 'special' or one-off but it was not commonplace. When Creed introduced the tailored suit as a fashionable item, however, all the most fashionable women of Europe had to have one.

The head or tailleur in the tailoring workroom in a couture house is usually a man who utilises all the precise methods of tailoring but converts them into the procedures and fashion feel of a couture house (see Chapter 1). Here, it is the designer who sets the scene – unlike the male tailors where the tailor and the client discuss the look, fit and fabric choice and between them decide on the 'design'. In the haute couture fashion sense this would not be called a design. After being directed by the designer or couturier on how the new design should be translated and cut, the couture tailor produces a toile or prototype for the designer to approve. This is fitted, adjusted and agreed on the model for fit, line, proportion and balance and then cut out in the cloth. The pieces are then tacked together and prepared for a further fitting. After all the adjustments have been made it is sewn together, lined, finished and buttonholed.

The couture women's tailor and the men's tailor, although in essence the same, have, over time, evolved as different practitioners: a craftsman in the world of men's tailoring would not be able to work in a couture house and vice versa. As women's tailoring became more and more part of mainstream fashion by the late 19th and early 20th centuries, every couture house would show a large tailoring section in each collection. Some couturiers became particularly known for their tailoring. Even those known for their soft flowing (flou) dresses were obliged to include at least some coats and suits in their day-wear. Molyneux, Balenciaga and Yves Saint Laurent considered tailoring as the highest form of haute couture and today Christian Lacroix and Karl Lagerfeld continue to include a large tailoring section in each collection.

Top left: a woman's tailor-made of 1890–1900, very much based on the tailoring for women introduced by Henry Creed.

Top right: a suit by Cristobal Balenciaga of the late 1940s showing his roots in tailoring.

This suit by Brioni from a showing in the Sala Bianca of the Pitti Palace in Florence in 1956 typifies the suave chic of the Italian tailors of the time. (From G.B. Giorgini Archive.)

A selection of silk ties by Emilio Pucci, late 1960s/early 1970s.

Chapter 5
Menswear

*Definition of menswear (wholesale tailoring) – The British tradition – Tailoring
for the masses –The middle market – The effect of market forces on
manufacturing – Specialist, patented and branded items – America – The Italian
influence – Menswear and the 1960s fashion revolution – Designer menswear –
Itinerant tailors and the rag trade – Men's ready-to-wear today*

Definition of menswear (wholesale tailoring)

Just as womenswear divides into couture, ready-to-wear and mass production so too does menswear. Bespoke tailoring equates with couture, whilst wholesale tailoring, which encompasses both ready-to-wear and mass production, is a specific industry. The whole fashion industry divides into two distinct camps: the dress industry and the tailoring industry. To the casual observer they might seem similar, but their cutting methods, manufacturing techniques and finishing methods are quite different.

The British tradition

Because of its tradition of great tailoring it seemed inevitable that Britain's wholesale menswear should have developed in that same tradition, and for a time it remained in this mould. The image and status of the City pinstripe three-piece suit was for many years the backbone of British, and especially English, middle-class dressing and therefore the model against which the market and middle-of-the-road menswear, both wholesale and retail, was gauged.

Tailoring for the masses

At the other end of the scale from the elite Savile Row tailors, two self-made men, Montague Burton of Burton's, and Henry Price of the Fifty Shilling Tailor, changed the face of British tailoring by providing a tailored suit for the man in the street at a price he could afford.

Most men could not afford to have a made-to-measure suit from either a local town or city tailor let alone from Savile Row, and for the average man this method of acquiring a suit was not for him but for the 'upper classes'. The man in the street could not afford the bespoke prices and would have felt awkward and out of his depth ordering and being measured for a suit. Burton's and the Fifty Shilling Tailors were the answer – off-the-peg suits and partially made-to-measure suits that involved the minimum alteration, available in a high street store, were much less expensive and less daunting. It became part of the working- and lower-middle-class culture to have a best suit, later through wear to be relegated to the working suit, a uniform in war time, a ***demob suit*** at the end of the war and probably a suit for weddings and funerals. All these were often bought from one or other of these giant establishments, although others such as Hector Powe and John Collier were close rivals. It must be remembered that the idea of hiring a morning suit from Moss Brothers and other hire firms and aping society weddings is a fairly recent phenomenon.

Montague Burton

Montague Burton was a Russian Jew born in 1885 in Kurkel, a town in the Russian province of Kovo, later Lithuania. His real name was Meshe David Osinsky and he emigrated to Leeds in England in 1900. As Morris Burton 'hosier and draper' he took premises at 20 Holywell Street in Chesterfield – he may have taken his new name from the nearby town of Burton-on-Trent. This little shop sold suits, shirts and caps, and these ready-mades sold at very low prices: eleven shillings and ninepence (58 pence) for a brown tweed suit for example.

By dint of hard work his business thrived. In 1908 he opened another shop in Mansfield market and in 1909 a premises in Sheffield and acquired works at Progress Mills in Leeds. After marrying Sophia Marks, the daughter of a local furniture dealer, in 1909, he became naturalised in 1910 as a British subject with the name of Morris Burton – Montague was a later addition. In 1914 he opened a further eight shops so that by the outbreak of World War I he had a total of fourteen shops. An expansion programme in 1915 added another five shops, with a further one in the following year in Wandsworth, London. This was a breakthrough, for not only was this his first shop in London but it was also a move upmarket and a change from his former policy of catering for the working class in poorer areas.

Making uniforms and securing good military contracts further advanced the business, so that at the end of the war when four million men needed civilian clothing again, Burton was able to supply this need. From 40 shops in 1919, by 1939 Montague Burton owned 505 shops. In 1921, the manufacturing side of the business was carried out in a newly built factory in Leeds where Burton introduced mass market

The British tradition; the typical London City 'gent' wearing a pinstripe single-breasted three-piece suit with bowler hat, spats and raincoat in 1924.

manufacturing methods. By 1925 this was the largest clothing factory in Europe.

In 1932 Montague Burton was knighted. Burton became a household word – 'the full Monty', using his acquired first name, was the working man's expression for being dressed up on Saturday night.

The menswear tailoring business expanded to the degree where it was able to take on and buy out many clothing companies, women's as well as men's. By 1998, when the giant Burton Group Plc changed its name to Arcadia, it included Burton Menswear, Dorothy Perkins, Evans, Hawkeshead, Principles, Racing Green, Top Shop and Top Man. In 1999 it acquired the Sears womenswear business including Miss Selfridge, Wallis, Warehouse and Outfit. At this point the Arcadia group owned 11.5% of the UK womenswear market.

Henry Price

Henry Price, born in Leeds in 1877, began his professional life at the age of 12 working in a clothing shop and later became a tailor and then manager of the Grand Clothing Hall in Keighley, Yorkshire. Together with his wife Ann Elizabeth Craggs, whom he married in 1899, he set up a market stall selling gentlemen's accessories. From their first small shop, opened in 1906, grew a huge tailoring empire with 500 outlets employing 12,000 people. He was one of the first to apply mass production methods to clothing production and consequently was able to sell quality suits for fifty shillings (£2.50), thus the sobriquet 'The Fifty Shilling Tailor', as the company became known. In order to satisfy his voracious and ever demanding business, for two years in a row he bought the entire Australian wool fleece output. During World War II his factories were responsible for supplying British troops with service uniforms and later their demob suits.

Price was knighted in 1939 and became the quintessential English gentleman, acquiring the estate of Wakehurst Place in West Sussex, with a fine Elizabethan mansion.

The middle market

In the middle ground of menswear in Britain, Austin Reed and Simpson's of Piccadilly offered an opportunity for middle-class men to buy good quality, well-tailored clothes 'off-the-peg'. Men that would never consider buying their suit from Burton's or the Fifty Shilling Tailor and could not really afford Savile Row tailoring looked to these companies for smart, high quality clothing.

Austin Reed

Austin Leonard Reed, born in 1873, was the second son of William Reed, partner in his father's firm, Thomas Reed and Son, hatters and hosiers of Reading. Early training from his father, a stint in London as 'cash boy' for a firm of hosiers in Ludgate Hill in the City of London and a most conciliatory spell as a junior with Wanamaker's of Philadelphia proved invaluable to his future career. Wanamaker's was at the time (1893) the world's largest retail outlet where he had a taste of bulk purchasing, retail pricing, window display and how mail order was organised. His experience was further widened by working in New York at Hackett, Carhart and Co., clothiers and furnishers, and in Chicago for Lincoln Bartlett, menswear importers. This early training led to a very sophisticated approach to menswear, marketing, manufacture and retailing. Building up from his first small shop in the City of London in Fenchurch Street in 1906 to much larger premises in the same street, he then acquired a sizeable warehouse in Nicholl Square. By 1911 it was time to venture out of the City, and Reed bought 113 Regent Street. He then acquired menswear businesses in Birmingham and Manchester. With the rebuilding of Regent Street in 1927 the old premises there were exchanged for the huge Regent Street store familiar to Londoners today. The many branches of Austin Reed are a feature of provincial towns throughout Britain.

Simpson

Simeon Simpson started Simpson in 1894 in a rented room in Middlesex Street, better known as Petticoat Lane, on the borders of the City and the East End of London. This area was a centre of the then garment trade, specialising in second-hand clothing and ready-made suits and trousers. Earning a reputation for high quality tailoring, Simpson soon increased his market and was able to take on staff, which he trained up to his own meticulous standard of workmanship.

Taking advantage of a revolution in mechanisation in the tailoring industry, the powered sewing machine, the all-important band knife, powered by gas and then by electricity, which enabled the cutter who previously cut out single layers of cloth with hand shears to cut many layers at once, Simpson realised early on that tailoring did not have to rely on individual craftwork; quality tailoring could be produced in quantity on the production line without a lowering of his high standards in make. Simpson introduced machinery for making buttonholes, sophisticated pressing equipment and production-line methods. He was so successful in this enterprise that he was able to open several factories in London and subsequently retail outlets throughout Britain and even abroad. He had a magnificent modern department store in Piccadilly and a manufacturing company with the brand name of DAKS.

The effect of market forces on manufacturing

Many British menswear companies who were primarily retail operators, such as Austin Reed, Marks and Spencer, and Simpson of Piccadilly, started up their own manufacturing companies

Formal tailcoat and single-breasted dinner jacket advertise a good quality London wholesale tailor in 1929.

to supply their stores – Chester Barrie at Austin Reed, St Michael at Marks and Spencer, and DAKS at Simpson are well-known examples. In recent years, however, they have had to rethink these operations. Retail and wholesale, by their very nature, work on two different timescales, with wholesale a year ahead of retail in producing the goods but the impact of sales hitting the retailer first. Any slowing down in market

Left: eveningwear from Simpson of Piccadilly 1938.

Below: these are 'stock blocks', that is everyday style patterns that manufacturers could buy to produce basic tailored items for the man in the street from the *Tailor and Cutter* 1948.

demand is therefore more obvious to the retailer, and having in-house wholesale manufacturing units has lately proved a less flexible method than *buying in* from abroad. Domestic manufacturing cannot compete with its rivals in the Far East either on price or on efficiency, and consequently some of these companies have had to sell off the manufacturing parts of their businesses.

Specialist, patented and branded items

As with so much in the clothing industry, it is the invention or development of a particular specialist item on which the fortunes of a brand depend, be it Robert Baker's ruff, the *Mackintosh*, the *Burberry*, Dr Jaeger's healthy underwear, Austin Reed's Summit collar, Lilywhite's sportswear or the Brooks Brothers' shirt, to name but a few.

The discovery in the middle of the 19th century of a tree that could produce a waterproof and malleable substance called rubber had a huge impact on many aspects of life, not least in the invention of the pneumatic tyre, but also in the process of coating fabrics to make them waterproof. Not strictly tailoring, but with a huge influence on menswear items throughout the world was Burberry's with its revolutionary waterproof Gabardine, first a name for a cloth but later the name for a garment – a raincoat. Apparently it was Edward VII who christened it – in saying, 'pass me my Gabardine'.

The influence of sportswear has always been great. Many items that start out as sportswear become, in time, menswear classics – the hunting hacking jacket is the model for today's sports jacket, the Norfolk jacket created for Edward VII to shoot in became in the 1920s and 1930s a casual piece of clothing, and the safari jacket meant for hunting game in Africa became a fashion item, so beloved of Yves Saint Laurent.

It was logical therefore that companies such as Burberry, Lilywhite's, Aquascutum and Jaeger that originated as sportswear specialists should become major suppliers of menswear to the British middle-class market.

America

In America, where a youthful, sporty, off-the-peg style had always predominated, Brooks Brothers cornered the Ivy League market, a market not necessarily made up of those who had gone to one of the ivy-clad universities of Yale and Harvard but which had consisted of those who had style aspirations towards a 'preppy', unstructured, youthful style of dress. No padding or interlining, soft natural shoulders, shorter trousers, button-down collared shirts and penny loafers were part of this easy dressing style. Surprisingly, Brooks are said to have based the style on the English look and it was after a visit to an English polo match that one of the brothers introduced the button-down collared shirt, a feature of English polo shirts, which became a hallmark of Brooks.

The Ivy League was just one of Brooks Brothers' markets. They catered to several layers of American society, including the old and newly rich. They also supplied those women who wanted tailoring such as Greta Garbo and Katherine Hepburn.

Henry Sandys Brooks had opened his first store as early as 1818 in order, as he said, 'to make and deal in merchandise of the finest quality to sell it at a fair profit and to deal with people who seek and appreciate such merchandise'. Henry Brooks Jr took control of the company in 1833, and in 1850 his sons, Daniel, John and Elisha, took over. It was from these three that Brooks Brothers took its world famous name.

Many influences have been attributed to America, not least that of Hollywood. The style and dressing of its male stars, many of whom actually had their suits made in Savile Row and wore them on screen, had a huge influence on the dressing habits of the American public. What originally was called the 'London cut' by those

From Jaeger, these five styles of 1934 characterise the casual, more sporty style that typified the brand.

Good wholesale tailoring from 1955: left, a tuxedo or double-breasted dinner jacket, and right, a lightweight single-breasted sports jacket.

This edge-to-edge, single button, shawl collared, dinner jacket is from Harrods in 1964. Worn with a black tie, cummerbund and suitable accessories, an alternative white tie and white waistcoat for more formal eveningwear is also illustrated.

A Hector Powe double-breasted suit from a 1963 advertisement.

'in the know' became popularly known as the 'American cut'. Inevitably, the huge menswear manufacturing giants of America copied these ideas in their millions. Sportswear, that forte of American casual wear, took on many guises, whether easy tailoring, preppy, fraternity, Italian or Hawaiian style. All had their influence on international menswear both in style, mass production and marketing techniques.

The Italian influence

Ever since rich 18th century English aristocrats had their portraits painted by Batoni in Rome while on their grand tour wearing luscious silks and taffetas, Italian men's dressing has been synonymous with high style and the relationship and rivalry between English and Italian tailoring has existed. However, it was not until the 1950s that this style had a real impact on world fashion. In about 1959 Italian fashion hit London and New York. In London, tailors, sometimes Italian sometimes not, made Italian-style suits, short boxy jackets or 'bum freezers', and straight, no turn-up trousers. It has been said that these very short jackets were made for riding Vespa scooters. Wide, square, slightly 'draped' shoulders superseded the Teddy Boy look. In New York and California the 'imported' Italian suit, like those worn by Frank Sinatra, Dean Martin and the rest of the 'Rat Pack', was *de rigueur* for film stars and society personalities.

By the late 1970s and early 1980s the influence of Giorgio Armani on world style and particularly on men's tailoring cannot be overestimated. The easy but sinuous fit, lack of padding and lightweight interlinings were a revolution in menswear (the more robust interlining and padding being so much a part of the tailoring ethic until this innovation). His ubiquitous low cut **revers** and much lower **notch** influenced collar and lapel cutting for the next decade in both men's and women's tailoring. In many ways it was Armani who persuaded the rich man that his suit need no longer be made to measure in order to be stylish. Armani's impeccable cutting, light superfine fabrics and huge choice of elegant styles made bespoke tailoring seem very dated. Armani wrote in 1996: 'The true leader of fashion is industry. Prêt à porter, the manufactured garment, is the true force of fashion. Today fashion is that which is sold in great quantities, or at least in quantities that are visible when you walk down the street. High fashion for the wealthy and the very rich still exists, but the rule is that the articles shown on the runway, with a few corrections and a few modifications, must be capable of becoming clothes for everyone.' Like Creed in the 19th century, Armani repopularised the tailored suit for women – no self-respecting woman executive could be without her chalk stripe Armani or Armani-inspired suit with its long, super-flattering jacket, short skirt, low cut revers and gentle, androgynous overtones.

Many Italian womenswear designers now include a menswear collection: Romeo Gigli and Moschino in the 1980s, Versace and Dolce and Gabbana in the 1990s, and Prada and Gucci today. Menswear designers like Etro, Iceberg and the comeback of Roberto Cavalli are extending the list of Italian menswear designers each year. Italy has taken the lead in men's ready-to-wear worldwide, and it is interesting to note that non-Italians such as Vivienne Westwood, Calvin Klein, Dirk Bikkembergs and Burberry have decided to show their menswear collections in Milan.

Menswear and the 1960s fashion revolution

No area could have been more affected by London's 1960s fashion revolution than menswear. Almost overnight the British male changed from being perhaps the most conservative dresser in the world to become a peacock. The same factors that influenced womenswear influenced menswear: sexual liberation, music, art and drugs. A vast selection of retail outlets,

mostly in Carnaby Street and the King's Road, Chelsea, catered for this ravenous market. A small vanguard of shops like Vince, just off Carnaby Street, blossomed into a plethora of shops, stores, unisex boutiques, stalls and markets. In Carnaby Street, John Stephen, Lord John and Take Six dealt with the cheaper end of the market whilst the King's Road and Kensington High Street attracted a slightly more up-market clientele. Places like Just Men, Village Gate and Vernon Lambert in Chelsea had such an influence on the male buying public that Austin Reed found it had to change its image – The Cue Shop at Austin Reed, the brainchild of Colin Woodhead, became the pattern for others such as Way In at Harrods.

Designer menswear

The really great change in menswear that happened in the 1960s was that it began to be designed. Before this it evolved: a jacket was shortened, revers were lengthened, a waist was made looser and a trouser leg was narrowed. It was the French designer Pierre Cardin who put the seal of approval on designed menswear with his 'cylinder line', which he launched on 26 February 1960 at the Crillon Hotel in Paris. Ted Lapidus, another French womenswear designer, followed suit in 1962, and he was followed in turn by most of the established Paris houses. The impact of Yves Saint Laurent's first menswear Rive Gauche ready-to-wear collection in 1969 was immense – he, together with Cardin, completely changed the market and the public's attitude towards men's fashion.

Itinerant tailors and the rag trade

As previously touched on, itinerant tailors had their roots in the Jewish communities where, because they were so often moved from place to place and from ghetto to ghetto, they needed a trade that was easily transportable. Tailoring only really required a needle and a pair of shears

Printed shirt and cut velvet
trousers for Just Men of the
King's Road, Chelsea, *ca.* 1967.

'Heathcliff', a romantic menswear
outfit for Bellville Sassoon
featured in *Women's Wear Daily*
in 1968.

and could be carried out anywhere squatting cross-legged on the floor. Jewish tradition has it that the Jews' talent for producing violinists was for similar reasons; the violin is also very portable. Once these communities did settle, they set up working areas that later became known as the rag trade centres of the world, and it was here too that the notorious sweat shops were to be found. These centres were the East End in London, Seventh Avenue in New York and Le Sentier in Paris. It is therefore not surprising that these areas became synonymous with the garment industry in all its forms.

Men's ready-to-wear today

The huge men's ready-to-wear establishment, with a calendar of shows in Paris, Milan, London and New York, today competes with womenswear. The designers may be womenswear designers who also design menswear or they may exclusively design menswear. New specialist menswear designers have been brought in to design menswear ranges for established fashion houses, and the number of ready-to-wear collections shown is growing each year. In 2003, there were 19 ready-to-wear menswear collections showing in Paris, 29 in Milan (now the favourite menswear ready-to-wear venue), seven in New York and seven in London, a lot of designers.

The difference between the traditional dressing of the London City businessman described at the beginning of this chapter and the garments shown today on the catwalk at the ready-to-wear menswear shows could not be more marked. The component parts are the same – a jacket, a pair of trousers and a shirt – but the attitude to menswear design has changed and so has the customer. Now the influence of fashion together with the power of branding make the modern man demand something different from his wardrobe. For designer menswear companies to be so prolific (nearly 70 companies showing

in Milan, Paris, London and New York, and this is the very top end of the market) it must mean that designer menswear is selling at a phenomenal rate, which in turn must mean that men's buying habits have changed. The explosion in men's fashion-conscious buying today is certainly equal to that seen in the 1960s but has quite a different slant – now it is driven by high-powered marketing and the all-powerful branding techniques.

Most designer ready-to-wear houses now show a separate menswear collection, usually designed by a specialist, unnamed menswear designer. There are exceptions, however: Hedi Slimane, first at Yves Saint Laurent and now at Christian Dior, or Naoki Takizama at Issey Miyake, or designers like Dirk Bikkembergs who are exclusively menswear designers and run their own house. These menswear collections are of similar size to womenswear collections, between 50 and 100 items, although Giorgio Armani showed as many as 170 items in the spring/summer 2003 collections in Milan, and Strenesse only 25. Jil Sander, taken over by Prada, now shows in Milan instead of Paris. Jean-Paul Gaultier, naturally still showing in Paris, showed about 50 items and, perhaps more surprisingly, the British designer Paul Smith showed 80 in Paris. Designer menswear shows no signs of diminishing and, at the present rate and with such an establishment of marketing experts, branding specialists and a calendar of international shows to support, it is likely to grow even further.

The great influence over the last few years has been that perennial impetus, sportswear. However, now the sports are somewhat different – snowboarding, skateboarding and football are more likely to inspire the younger designers. Variations on classic menswear are still popular currency with designers like Ralph Lauren, Calvin Klein and Paul Smith, and, although in a different league, Hugo Boss, the Stuttgart giant, could be called the businessman's Armani.

A Dries Van Noten design from the 2003 spring/summer Paris men's collection held at the Allée des Cygnes.

Also from Dries Van Noten, a design from the 2003 spring/summer Paris men's collection.

A bourgeois dressmaking establishment, *The Dressmaker's Shop in Arles* by Antoine Ruspal (1738–1811), mid to late 18th century. The woman on the left already takes on the role of première de l'atelier and directs her hands from a position of authority.

Chapter 6
Dressmaking

*The origins of dressmaking – Dressmaking as part of traditional female education –
Dressmaking as a career – Paper patterns – Levels of dressmaking –
The difference between the dress industry and the dressmakers' craft*

The origins of dressmaking

The crafts of dressmaking and tailoring have been known in some form from early history, and in medieval times garment-makers formed trade or craft associations or guilds. Because of the strictures of the early guilds, run by men, all medieval garment-making, whether for men or for women, was carried out by men. The real origins of dressmaking as a female craft are difficult to ascertain as all *making* of outer garments was a male prerogative and kept as such – a strict code of conduct overseen by the guild brothers.

From a very early period, travelling or journeymen tailors operated a system whereby they visited villages and outlying settlements, took orders and delivered these orders made up in due course. Precisely how these early journeymen operated is unknown. Whether they carried samples, how they took measurements, how the cloth was woven and ordered is an area ripe for research. Much later, the male dressmaker, known as a *mantuamaker*, was allowed to employ his wife and daughters as seamstresses. Professional mantua or dressmakers even in the remoter towns of Scotland would visit London to buy models to copy as early as 1660. The term 'mantuamaker' derives from the French *manteau* meaning loose outer garment and continued in use well into the 20th century as mantle maker, a term often seen in advertisements or outfitters' shop-fronts. The practice of circulat-ing fashion dolls or poupées dressed in the latest fashion from which customers could order items is thought to have started as early as the 16th century. The proof for this is said to be the depiction of fashionably dressed dolls in portraits of that time. The word 'mannequin' comes from this idea of dolls or mannequins displaying samples for the client's approval from which orders could be taken.

At first, only widows or daughters of the established tailor or mantuamaker were allowed to take over established businesses, but by the 18th century dressmaking had become a predominately female occupation. Previously, only underwear and children's clothes had been the province of 'the weaker sex', as they were considered at the time.

Dressmaking as part of traditional female education

The tradition of dressmaking as part of female education, both in the home and at school, has now gone; it is now only remembered by the older generation. Domestic science was a major part of the curriculum of all girls' secondary schools and dressmaking and cooking skills were its main subjects. The so-called innate skills patronisingly attributed to the female population meant that, when it came to careers, dressmaking, together with cooking and domestic service were considered the natural choices for girls.

Dressmaking as a career

Dressmaking was a career that could be carried out from home, and professional home dressmakers usually visiting customers in their own houses could thus achieve a reasonably successful business. A business built up in this way gave the dressmaker a status higher than that of a domestic servant. However, for a higher quality of workmanship it was necessary for the aspiring dressmaker either to attend a trade school or to buy an apprenticeship with an established dressmaking company. If she had exceptional skill she could be apprenticed to a couture house – many of the great women couturières started their careers in this manner. Gabrielle Chanel and Jeanne Lanvin are good examples.

My own English middle-class grandmother would employ a live-in dressmaker who would come to stay for a season each year to make all the children's clothes and most of her own work-a-day clothes. This was a tradition she took over from her own mother and was probably a fairly normal occurrence for that type of family.

Every town and village must have had many home dressmakers. In the census returns of the mid 19th century, dressmaking is one of the most common occupations for the daughters of the family. In large towns of this period, hundreds of women were employed in the larger dressmaking establishments which sprang up to supply the growing and affluent middle-class market, and in the workrooms of both large and medium-sized department stores where their skills as *alteration hands* were constantly in demand. The trade directories of Britain's large towns and cities advertised such dressmaking establishments at all levels of status and quality.

The dressmaker's reputation in society has varied from the very respectable spinster of village or small town life to the often undeserved dubious reputation of the Parisian dressmaker often thought of as a *midinette* – a girl of 'easy virtue'. At the end of the 19th century there were thousands of dressmakers in the City of Paris and more women were employed in this trade than in any other including domestic service.

Paper patterns

A huge selection of paper patterns was available for the home dressmaker and even the professional dressmaker. These could be bought in every kind of retail outlet, from the huge department store to the village post office. Making one's own clothes was simply a part of everyday life and most homes had a domestic sewing machine, an item no longer part of the furniture as it was even 20 years ago. Most women's magazines of the time supplied either paper patterns within the magazine or diagrams from which the reader could construct her own. Vogue, Butterick, Weldon and many other suppliers of paper patterns also carried huge catalogues of their styles at reasonable prices. A model pattern, one bought from a well-known couturier by the paper pattern publisher to be copied by home dressmakers, could be very expensive and these copies were the mainstay not only of publications like *Vogue Pattern Book* but also in some cases of the couturier, who received not only a fee for the original design but also a royalty on the number of patterns sold.

Retail fabric departments in department stores and specialist 'material' retailers were a major element of the high street and the average woman's trip to town included buying cloth which she would either make up herself or farm out to a dressmaker. In London the *fabric halls* of Harrods, Dickens and Jones, D.H. Evans, Marshall and Snelgrove, and John Lewis were emporiums of textile delights, stocking a huge diversity of fabrics from all the best suppliers and manufacturers in the world. Today probably only John Lewis is left to give a taste of this former glory and is now, on the whole, used by semi-professionals.

Left and below left: a bed jacket and a pattern for it in a contemporary dressmaker's magazine offer of 1890.

DIAGRAM 8, REPRESENTING 36-INCH LINING, SHOWING HOW TO CUT OUT THE LINING YOKE FRONT AND BACK FOR NO. 16059, DRESSING JACKET.

Above: from a dressmaking magazine of 1899, a flat pattern offer for three styles for the home dressmaker.

95

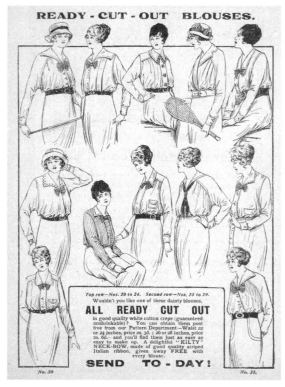

An example of the diversity of dressmaking enterprises – a pattern company offers cut-out blouses in fine quality cotton crepe with Italian ribbon for the necktie. All the home dressmaker had to do was to sew them up.

An advertisement for fabric from a woman's magazine, 1932.

An advertisement directed towards the semi-professional dressmaker in a woman's magazine of 1932.

Dressmakers!
Latest Fashionable Fabrics

On receipt of your Card or Billhead we will send you a selection of patterns free, or supply you with a large set for 1/- (which we refund with first order of 20/- or over) and will cut you

Any Length at Trade Price

Our Novelties for Autumn and Winter include:
Diagonals, Cords, Bouclés, Fancy Tweeds, Velours, Faced Cloths, Botany Wool Goods, Art. Silk Velvets, Velveteens, Art. Silk Fabrics, Winceys, Flannelettes, etc.

Tailor-made Coats to special measures, with Fur Collars, may be had in latest fashionable designs. Style and fit guaranteed.

Illustrated Catalogue of Fashions and Drapery Sent Free.

PLEASE ORDER YOUR PATTERN SET AT ONCE.

THE DRESSMAKERS' CLOTH CO., 5S, Armley, LEEDS.

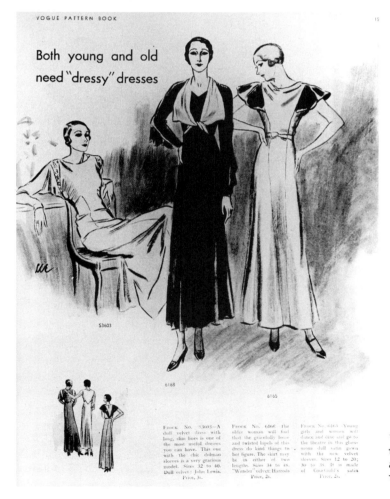

VOGUE PATTERN BOOK

Both young and old need "dressy" dresses

Vogue dress pattern of January 1933: the same basic shape with three alternatives – this is a typical format for pattern sales.

97

An advertisement for British fabric *ca.* 1935.

"Tricoline"

REGD. TRADE MARK NO. 585,732. *A Clemco Fabric*

The equal to Silk.

please! The BRITISH fabric.

Women trust instinctively in "Tricoline," the equal to silk. Use and launder it as they may, it remains as lovely as real silk. For dress and lingerie wear durable "Tricoline" is produced in the finest colours and stripe effects.

The genuine material bears the name "Tricoline" on the Selvedge. Genuine "Tricoline" garments have "Tricoline" tab affixed. "Tricoline" can be obtained by the yard and in garments ready to wear from leading Drapers throughout the country.

If any difficulty, please write to the Manufacturers, 5, Tricoline House, 16 Watling Street, London, E.C.4

N.C "Tricoline," WEATHERCOATS
Made and Proofed by Nicholson & Co., St. Albans. Rainproof yet porous. Light yet warm.

THE WEDDING PARTY

8331

An American wedding dress pattern of June 1935.

The front entrance of Harrods in the mid-1920s. Harrods had one of the most luxurious fabric halls in London.

Levels of dressmaking

In modern history the dressmaker and tailor have been of vital importance to all the aspiring classes. To be well dressed was always a measure of success: as Shakespeare says in *Hamlet*, Act I, scene 3: 'For the apparel oft proclaims the man'. This tradition continued well into the 20th century – even until World War II most people would use a tailor or dressmaker to make their best clothes.

There were many levels of quality: jobbing dressmakers, middling dressmakers, high quality dressmakers and court dressmakers whose standards could be extremely high but would not warrant being officially called a couturier. To be recognised as a couturier involved belonging to the modern equivalent of a guild, such as France's Chambre Syndicale de la Couture Parisienne (see Chapter 1). These were virtually exclusive clubs with very difficult entrance requirements and rigorous rules. One of the primary rules, for instance, of all the associations was originality of design. Most dressmakers or tailors copied existing designs either from models they had seen, from sketches or later on from

A skilled dressmaking operative in a modern factory.

photographs. Murray Arbeid, a traditional London dress designer who in the 1970s threw over his background and became a most successful ready-to-wear designer, says that in London, even during the 1950s and 1960s, there were hundreds of high class dressmaking establishments but, despite their levels of excellence and employment of a large staff quite equivalent to the great couture houses, they were never likely to be accepted by the Incorporated Society of London Fashion Designers as haute couturiers. The Minutes of the Society, held by the Victoria and Albert Museum, bear this out, recording how difficult it was to be accepted as a member and the number of times that very well known establishments of the time were turned down.

The difference between the dress industry and the dressmakers' craft

The dress industry, which is the major player in the vast global garment industry, has its roots in the craft of dressmaking, and it was by mechanising its manual procedures that the basis for modern-day volume production techniques was conceived. This is, in fact, the dress industry as opposed to the tailoring industry which, although similar in principle, is not the same. The dress industry produces all light clothing: dresses, blouses, skirts, shirts, trousers, nightwear and lingerie, but not bras which are part of the corsetry industry. Its working methods are different from those of tailoring – the patterns are different, the seam allowances are different, the finishing is different, the interlinings are different but above all the personnel is different. The dress industry is primarily a women's industry whereas tailoring is a men's. Men might be *production managers*, *stock cutters* and in some instances *cutters* in the dress industry but the bulk of the employees are women, the greatest number being the *machinists*.

The levels of dressmaking can be anything from *volume production* (as described above) to just one domestic worker working at home. They also operate on different levels of quality, from haute couture at the top end of the market to *sweat shop* manufacture at the lower end where millions of garments can be produced (see Chapter 3, Mass Production).

Chapter 7
Millinery and Accessories

The couturiers' ancillary trades – Millinery – Paris milliners – The millinery manufacturing process – The decline of the milliner – Buttons – Belts – Shoes – Embroiderers – Pleaters, buttonholers and pressers – Linings and interlinings

The couturiers' ancillary trades

Supporting the exclusive couture trade is a complex network of other trades whose industry and talent are vital to the maintenance and smooth running of haute couture. These are the milliners, the shoemakers, the belt makers, the embroiderers, the button makers, the braid makers, the corsetières, the hosiers, the furriers and the feather suppliers.

Paris was the original home of this complex network of highly skilled trades and the place where it reached the highest state of sophistication. The maintenance in luxury of the well-dressed woman from her lingerie (undergarments) to her fur coat, her modiste (milliner), her bottier (shoemaker), coiffure, stockings and even scent, were the responsibility of her couturier and his supporting entourage of these highly skilled ancillary trades whether in-house or by recommendation to an outside purveyor. Many of these formerly separate craft trades either became exclusively associated with a particular couturier or were absorbed into the house itself. Others remained specialist independent companies, such as Hermès, famous for its scarves, who became the darling of the English county set and who was in turn imitated worldwide. Scarves were also sold in the boutiques of the couturiers who asked great painters such as Picasso, Dali, Matisse, and fashionable illustrators like Bérard to design them. Today these have become collectors' items and are sold with paintings in international auction houses.

In England in 1957 members of these ancillary trades that had supported the London couturiers were accepted by the Incorporated Society of London Fashion Designers as associate members, and the Chambre Syndicale did the same for their ancillary trades.

Millinery

The great milliners were second only in importance to the great couturier designers in the hierarchy of the fashion world. This art is likened to sculpture because of its three-dimensional form and because it has to work from every angle. The three levels of couture, ready-to-wear and mass production apply to this discipline just as much as to the rest of fashion. On the highest level the haute couture milliner, known as the modiste, held immense sway. Rose Bertin, that great arbiter of style and Queen Marie-Antoinette's 'minister of fashion', was in fact a milliner (see Chapter 8).

Paris was the home of the hat: even Cole Porter acknowledged this in his famous line 'if a Harris pat means a Paris hat', from the 1948 Broadway musical, *Kiss Me, Kate*. While London and New York had their celebrated masters of the art, many of these had French origins or training. In London, Simone Mirman and Rose Vernier were French and worked with London's 'top ten' couturiers and were associate

A fashionable hat of 1780 indicative of the kind of hat that Rose Bertin would have designed and stocked in her millinery shop in Paris.

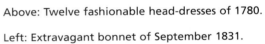

Above: Twelve fashionable head-dresses of 1780.

Left: Extravagant bonnet of September 1831.

'Fashions for June' from Belle Assemblée 1839 – bonnets with a 17th century feel, which was part of a romantic revival at this time.

Left: Caroline Workman in a frivolous, ruffled mob cap *ca.* 1899.

Right: ten years later she wears a severe and elegant felt hat with a veil.

members of the Incorporated Society; Otto Lucas was German but had worked in Paris before setting up in Mayfair in 1932; and Aage Thaarup, who was Danish, was for many years the royal milliner, a position held today by Frederick Fox. The great New York milliners were: Lily Daché, born in France but who set up in New York in 1924 and was apprenticed to the celebrated Paris milliner Reboux; Mr John, a German who had briefly worked in Paris and opened in New York in 1929; and Adolopho from Cuba who opened his own New York house in 1962.

Paris milliners

The great Paris milliners, although not household names like the great couturiers, are to the initiated the inspiration for world millinery. Until 1964, Albouy had a house at 49 rue de Colisée. Jean Barthet who presented his first collection in 1949 achieved international fame making hats for the Hollywood stars and designed the hats for such films as *Demoiselle de Rochefort*. Jeanne Blanchot, who was also a sculptor, was a milliner from 1910 to 1959 and worked in Faubourg Saint Honoré; she was for a time the president of the Chambre Syndicale. Simone Cange, who worked on her own before joining Claude St-Cyr, became the milliner to Carven. Jeanne Le Monnier was born in Paris in 1887 and opened her house at 231 rue Saint Honoré in 1921; it did not close until 1954. Known for her supple working of embroidery and découpage into her creations, she numbered many great French actresses as her clients. Maud

and Nano, as première and seconde at the famous old house of Suzy, opened their own house in 1942, which continued until 1964. Giving up his studies of the organ at the Schola Cantorum, Gilbert Orcel followed his talent for making hats, which had started at the age of five. In 1938 he created memorable hats for an exhibition at the Petit Palais and after the 1945 Liberation his work received international acclaim.

Paulette, who set up in 1939 in Avenue Franklin Roosevelt, found fame in 1942 as the creator of the 'cycling turban', a practical item of clothing, which became very popular with Parisian women during the Occupation. She continued as milliner to many of the great couturiers. Caroline Reboux, milliner since the Second Empire, opened her house at 23 rue de la Paix in 1870; the house continued later under the direction of Lucienne Rebaté until well into the second half of the 20th century. Claude Saint-Cyr opened in 1937 working in conjunction with Jean Patou at 122 rue du Faubourg St. Honoré showing collections in London and Tokyo, and her name became a byword for French fashion. Svend, who had worked for Jacques Fath from 1947 to 1951, set up his own house at 50 rue de Ponthieu where he created hats for the couturiers Jacques Heim and Pierre Balmain. Suzanne Talbot who was both couturière and milliner set up her house at 14 rue Royale in 1907 – after World War II she moved to Avenue Matignon, closing in 1956. Rose Valois, who trained with Reboux, opened her house in 1927 at 18 rue Royale and closed in 1970.

Five examples of Parisian millinery from September 1924 from *Femina*. Top left: two cloche hats trimmed with lacquered feathers by Jane Blanchot. Top right: hat in velvet by Georgette trimmed with a pompom in three shades of violet. Centre: again by Georgette, a large hat trimmed with ostrich plumes. Bottom right: by Collot, a black toque with a long mourning veil. Bottom left: again by Jane Blanchot, a velvet turban and a velvet hat trimmed with black faille.

A copy in black felt of a model of the great French milliner Caroline Reboux by Eve Valère of the late 1920s.

Above: a straw hat trimmed with ostrich feathers by the great Paris milliner Paulette. Left: a draped, spotted net hat by another great Paris milliner Svend. Both *ca.* 1955.

The millinery manufacturing process

A hat is a three-dimensional object and has to be formed like a piece of sculpture – the test for a good hat, according to Parisian model milliners of the 1930s, was that it should look right from every angle. Model hats are designed in the fabric or *sparterie* either on the head or on a head dummy. The traditional fabrics for millinery are felt and straw; these can be trimmed with net, flowers, feathers or fur, but a hat can be made in any material from dress fabric to a confection made only of net veiling. Felt comes in pre-formed *hoods*, that is a felt shape already taking the rough shape of a hat, either a *cloche* or bell shape or a *caplin*, a crown and brim shape. The *crown* and the *brim* are the basic components from which all hats are constructed – the crown fitting over the crown of the head and the brim – a circle with a hole in it – fitting the circumference of the head. *Peaks* are related to the brim, being of course a section of a circle. Felts are made of wool or fur fibres 'felted' rather than woven in order to make them particularly pliable and plastic so that they can be moulded into a three-dimensional shape. In order to do this the felt hood or caplin has to be moulded with steam over a *hat block*, made of wood in model millinery but of metal in mass production. Straws can be, like felts, pre-formed hoods or caplins, but can also come in the form of a continuous ribbon called *strip straw*, which can be machined together to form a shape.

Millinery for the woman in the street was unlikely to mean a hat from one of the great French milliners. It could, however, mean a copy of a French model hat from the local millinery shop bought and trimmed in-house or bought direct from one of the huge hat manufacturers. Between the modiste and the wholesale hat industry were the 'model' hat makers where copies of Paris styles were made by hand but in great numbers by an army of milliners which in the past could be found in every city and provincial town. These representatives of the hat trade were often found where a similar trade had been based in the past. In England, straw plait had been made since the 18th century in Luton which became the centre of the British hat trade. At its height, Luton could boast as many as 20 hat factories. This meant that it was the centre not only for making hats but also for all the trades associated with it: *block makers*, *felt makers*, *straw plaiters*, *flower makers* and feather suppliers.

The decline of the milliner

The advent of the hair stylist in the 1960s, and probably in particular Vidal Sassoon, spelt the end of the hat as an everyday item. A huge wholesale industry employing thousands of workers was brought to its knees by this change in fashion; Luton, for example, had to close many of its famous factories including Reslaw (Paul Walser), Bermona (Bermans) and Fitzroy Biggs. It was not only an industry that was ruined, in many ways the art was lost too. Only Frederick Fox, the royal milliner, Graham Smith and Phillip Somerville really survived in London and were able to cash in on a new interest in hats in the 1980s. In the 1980s and 1990s, new stars such as Stephen Jones and Philip Treacy arrived on the scene and did for millinery what Galliano and McQueen did for fashion. Jones, a St Martin's graduate, created the hats for Jean-Paul Gaultier's and Thierry Mugler's collections, and Treacy designs the hats for Karl Lagerfeld at Chanel.

A mini Homburg in honey-coloured straw
and a straw boater, both from 1935.

The great model of the 1950s, Barbara Goalen, wears a felt hat
with a turn-back brim dated 1950.

A Philip Treacy couture hat from his couture show, July 2001.

Buttons

The buying public can often underestimate the importance of trimmings and accessories to the fashion world. The button industry, for instance, is large and sophisticated and involves research, design, highly skilled manufacture and distribution. Its markets are wholesale, retail and high fashion. The process starts from the raw materials; buttons can be made from both natural and man-made materials or a mixture of both. Bone, horn, tortoiseshell, mother of pearl, glass and metal were the traditional materials, but they have been superseded by nylon, plastic and polyurethane. Until quite recently the bulk of good quality buttons were made from casein, a hardened by-product of milk, with the qualities of bone which could be carved and moulded in a similar way.

Button manufacturers may specialise in a particular field: metal buttons for military uniforms, fashion buttons, practical heavy-duty buttons for workwear and other specialist tasks. The fashion button is, however, the most common, and companies producing this type of button will offer hundreds of styles with many new designs created for each season. Button manufacturers show their styles at fabric, fashion and product fairs so that the designers and clothing manufacturers can choose button styles for the coming season.

Button designs are shown on *button cards* and each card will represent a particular look – classics like tortoiseshell and pearl, and fancy shapes, together with buckles, clips and toggles. Most cards will have between 10 and 20 styles and companies will normally show 30 to 40 cards. Buttons have a method of sizing all their own measured in lignes (14–100); a one inch diameter button is, for example, 40 lignes. Designers such as Chanel and Saint Laurent have always had exclusive buttons, which have almost become part of their trademark.

Good designers will have prepared the way before starting to design a collection. Not only will they have attended fabric fairs, ordered first cloth samples, become aware of any *colour predictions* and *forecasts* but they will also have made sure that they have seen all the available button cards showing next season's button and buckle samples, belt designers' samples, embroiderers' swatches and new trimming notions.

Belts

Belt makers are another important adjunct to the creation of the fashion garment whether it be high fashion or workwear. The belt makers' trade originated in the craft of saddlery as do its sister industries, the luggage trade and the handbag manufacturer. The role of the belt maker who works exclusively for the fashion industry is slightly different. Belt makers show their current season's samples from which the designer makes a selection for the coming collection. On the other hand, the designer may design an entirely new style and require the belt maker to make a special sample of it. Either way, the liaison between the designer and the belt maker is a vital part of the design process.

Fashion belts can be in different kinds of leather – patent leather, snakeskin, hide or glove leather – or they can be made of plastic or fabric. Quite often a garment will need a *self* belt which is made in the same fabric as the dress, coat or suit. Specialist belt makers usually offer this service where the given fabric is mounted on to a specialised, stiffened base to form the belt, with the buckle also made of the fabric. The shape, width, length and character of the belt can be surprisingly varied: a belt can make or break an outfit. Belts can border on the craft of jewellery with chain belts, diamanté or

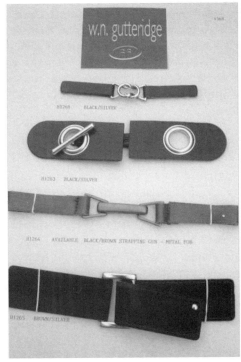

A button card and a belt card from which the designer can choose appropriate buttons or belts.

111

Above: A shoe collection from a wardrobe *ca.* 1890

Below: The famous Chanel sandal designed by René Mancini in 1954. Its modified version is still in use today.

rhinestone belts, and these would usually be made by another specialist in these techniques.

It is interesting to note how many of the most influential present-day fashion companies have their roots in saddlery or its sister industries belts and bags: Louis Vuitton, Gucci and Prada for instance.

Shoes

The design of shoes is such a huge subject that it cannot really be dealt with here in any depth. Suffice it to say that those designers that design specifically for the couturiers' collections, such as René Mancini who created the celebrated Chanel sandal or Roger Vivier who, from 1953, designed every shoe for the House of Dior, are an inestimable part of creating the total look of a collection. In Britain, the half Czech, half Spanish Manolo Blahnik has been designing spectacular shoes to international acclaim since the mid 1970s, and Jimmy Choo, who studied shoe design at London's Cordwainer's, has in the past few years gained a worldwide reputation.

Embroiderers

The art of embroidery has long been associated with the dress trade and even in the past with the tailor's profession. The 18th century embroidered waistcoat familiar to children through the story and illustrations of Beatrix Potter's *Tailor of Gloucester* is a good example.

It is still possible to find embroidered waistcoats and coat fronts in their un-made-up form, in other words the shapes traced out on one piece of flat material before they are cut out. This gives a good idea of professional embroidery production techniques. The areas to be decorated are prepared on a flat surface where, sometimes, the pattern pieces have been marked out in advance. The advantage of this is that the embroidery can be sent to a specialist embroidery workshop or outworker, stretched on a frame, the embroidery completed and returned to the dress company and then cut out and put together. Very often the pattern pieces need to be remarked as embroidery can cause the fabric to 'shrink'.

An embroidery designer will usually do many samples to show and discuss with the designer. These samples can be costed for time and materials. If, for instance, the embroidery is beaded, it is important to know how many beads of different types and colours will go into making a small ten centimetre square sample and therefore what beads would be needed for an entire garment. This cannot be done by guesswork but needs mathematical calculation.

The great embroidery design houses like Lesage in Paris have supplied the couturiers for many years and their dedication to the work and extraordinary craftsmanship is of world renown. François Lesage took over the company when his father Albert died in 1949. Lesage senior and his wife, fashion designer Marie-Louise Favot, had been developing this amazing company since 1924 which today is still successful and supplying the French designers with the highest quality embroidery. Swiss specialists can produce mechanical methods of reproducing high quality embroidery in bulk but the mass production manufacturers now look to the expert embroiderers of India and the Far East to reproduce really sumptuous effects at a comparatively low cost. Whichever method of production is used, the process is begun by the sampling. Embroidery can be in heavy wool or raffia or even using shells, for example in McQueen's 1998 collection. A woollen peasant embroidery could be produced in the country where this is part of the culture and appropriated by the fashion industry for a season; the next season the industry might want to look elsewhere. The whole cycle depends on fashion and what designers feel is right for that season.

Samples of ethnic and modern embroideries commissioned by Dries Van Noten for his spring/summer 2003 collection.

Pleaters, buttonholers and pressers

Although large mass production companies will have most of their process equipment 'in-house', smaller designer companies often need to send certain processes to specialist outworkers. The pleating companies are a good case in point. Pleaters can produce a great variety of pleating styles through steam or heat processes that 'bend' the fabric permanently. Box, knife, accordion, sun-ray, inverted, random and even the more complicated variations used by Issey Miyake can be accomplished by professional specialist pleaters and remain permanent as long as the fabric contains a certain proportion of man-made fibre. Natural fibres cannot be permanently pleated because the fibre cannot be 'bent'. This service greatly widens the scope of the smaller design company.

A similar service is Reece buttonholing. A really professional-looking buttonhole, almost identical to a hand-worked tailored buttonhole, can be achieved by using a Reece buttonholer. The machines are complicated and expensive to install for the smaller manufacturer, but again, specialist buttonhole companies offer a service where finished garments, appropriately marked, can be buttonholed off the premises as the process before pressing.

Even pressing can in some instances be carried out by a bought-in specialist, where an expert presser is called in by smaller companies usually for the final pressing of the sample collection before showing at presentations to buyers.

Linings and interlinings

The internal structure of a garment can be as important as the outside, whether it is structured or unstructured, lined or unlined. Usually, structure applies to tailored garments but the unlined quality and fluidity of a garment can be equally important, for example in the work of Madeleine Vionnet and Madame Grès who pioneered unlined, unstructured garments.

For the structured coat or suit jacket, the interlining, padding and lining are of great importance and can be very sophisticated. The principle for jackets and coats is taken from the practices of traditional men's tailors. Several layers of different types of interlining can be used to hold out or mould the shape, especially over the shoulder and chest. Different shapes of shoulder pads, depending on the shoulder shape required, enhance the shoulder line, which varies from season to season and is a major contributor to the fashion silhouette – Claude Montana's huge pads in the early 1980s influenced a generation. Traditional horsehair, collar, red-edge, heavyweight and lightweight canvases are used to achieve the structured shapes that bespoke tailors require, but huge technological advances have meant that, in ready-to-wear, much lighter interlinings can be used to achieve the same effect.

Goalen with a range of fashion accessories from the department store Harvey Nichols in 1950.

Chapter 8
The Designers

A minister of fashion and an official designer to the Revolution (Bertin and Leroy) – The father of haute couture (Worth) – The tailored suit for women (Creed) – New styles for a new century: the extravagant and the classic (Poiret and Molyneux) – Three powerful women: Chanel, Vionnet and Schiaparelli – Two opposing forces: the New Look and free form (Dior and Balenciaga) – The genius of the second half of the 20th century (Saint Laurent) – Casual classicism (McCardell, Muir and Rykiel) – New York style (Norell and Mainbocher) – The Sixties (Quant, Courrèges, Cardin, Biba, Rhodes and Clark)– New couture (Lagerfeld and Lacroix) – The renegades: James, Gaultier and Westwood – Italian high life and glamour (Carosa, Galitzine, Simonetta, Fabiani, Pucci, Fontana and Capucci) – Italian couture today (Valentino and Versace) – A new tailoring (Armani) – The Italian ready-to-wear designers (Albini, Dolce and Gabbana, Gigli, Gucci, Missoni, Moschino and Prada) – The impact of the Japanese (Kawakubo, Kenzo, Miyake and Yamamoto) – The Belgian force (Bikkembergs, Demeulemeester, Margiela, Thimster and Van Noten) – American simplicity (Jacobs, Karan, Klein, Kors and Lauren) – An Austrian and German duo (Lang and Sander) – All change (McCartney, Galliano, McQueen and Ford)

This brief history of designers is intended to give an outline of the key figures in the development of haute couture and ready-to-wear. This is not a comprehensive list but a list of those designers who in some way have changed either fashion, its perception or how the process works – technical innovations can be as important as design changes.

A minister of fashion and an official designer to the Revolution

Rose Bertin 1750–1812

Reputedly the first international fashion designer couturier, Bertin became the arbiter on dress to Queen Marie-Antoinette of France, the Czarina of Russia, much of the English aristocracy and even to the new rich of the newly independent America; she was the feared doyenne of dress for a generation.

Rose Bertin, Marie-Antoinette's 'minister of fashion'.

Originally a milliner, her extravagant head-dresses during Marie-Antoinette's period of influence were noted even in the literature of the time. It was her influence on the style of the queen that in fact dubbed her the minister of fashion and she was held partly responsible by the following regime (the Revolution) for the unfortunate queen's extravagance. Born Marie-Jeanne Laurent in Abbeville, Picardy, the daughter of a gendarme, she was sent to Paris as an apprentice to the milliner Pagalle. Here she so impressed the current leaders of fashion, the Princess Conti and the Duchess of Chartres, that they introduced her to the young dauphine, Marie-Antoinette, who had only just arrived at the sophisticated French court from Austria. It was through Bertin's influence that the queen developed her, later legendary, sense of style. Bertin's first shop, Au Grand Mogul, was opened in 1773 in the rue Saint Honoré and in 1787 she moved to rue de Richelieu. After the Reign of Terror she fled to Germany and later to England. In London she set up as a couturière and was able, through her earnings, to help émigrés and former clients to survive during their exile. She returned to Paris in 1800, not forgotten; she was able to set up business again in her old Paris shop until 1812 and is reported to have died in the autumn of that year.

Hyppolyte Leroy 1763–1829

Hyppolyte Leroy was known as Josephine's couturier; he dressed both of Napoleon's wives but had dressed Josephine before she became empress and designed for her elegant friends Thérèse Tallien and Madame Récamier during the difficult period of Revolution, Directoire and First Empire. The neo-classical style of dress prescribed by the Revolutionary Committee meant that Leroy had to design within these limits – limits set by the paintings of Jacques Louis David. However, the later luxurious style of the First Empire court allowed him scope for his extravagant ideas.

A print of a classical dress in the style of Leroy.

The son of a stagehand at the Paris Opera, Leroy was apprentice to a hairdresser there at the age of 12. He was later employed by Rose Bertin to work on headdresses for Marie-Antoinette, an opportunity that led to his becoming the queen's hairdresser. He survived the Revolution and in fact helped influence the Directoire look of the 1790s.

His long and successful career meant that he dressed the most important women of several regimes: Empress Josephine, Empress Marie-Louise and Countess Marie Walewska (Napoleon's Polish mistress). Leroy made the sumptuous coronation robes of both Emperor Napoleon and the restored king Charles X; the David painting of Napoleon's coronation is evidence of the brilliance of his work.

The father of haute couture

Charles Frederick Worth 1825–95

Worth was an Englishman who set up in Paris in the winter of 1857/58 and dressed all the most important women in the western world.

It is somewhat surprising that Charles Frederick Worth, the man considered by most people as the father of French couture, was English – called by Dame Nellie Melba, the opera diva and a customer, 'a Manchester boy'. In fact he came from a family of solicitors in Bourne, Lincolnshire, and kept his 'broad northern country accent' all his life. He is said to have served his apprenticeship at Swan and Edgar, a London *dry goods establishment*, later to become one of the capital's foremost department stores. Other sources say he started work at Lewis and Allenby, silk mercers who had a royal licence from Queen Victoria. Whatever the true sequence of his early working life, he developed and perfected his appreciation of the 'French milliner's and dress making skills' fairly early in his career. On leaving Lewis and Allenby with whom he kept in contact for many years he tried his luck in Paris, starting as a shop assistant at La Ville de Paris, another dry goods establishment, but was soon taken on as a selling clerk at Gagelin-Opigez et Cie. This large clothing company built its reputation on importing cashmere shawls and other luxury items from the East. By 1850, Worth is believed to have started creating or designing dresses for Gagelin-Opigez. He set up his own house in partnership with Otto Gustave Bobergh at the end of 1857 at 7 rue de la Paix with no more than 50 workers. A few years later it was said that the house employed more than a thousand including the outside workshops.

The house became the most important in the world with clients including the Empress Eugénie of France, the Queen of Norway, the Empress of Austria, Princess Pauline Metternich and legions of rich Americans who flocked to Paris to be dressed by the 'master'. Even Charles Dickens remarked sarcastically of the 'bearded Parisian milliner who held all society women in his sway'. Worth held his supremacy for two generations; he had two sons, Jean-Philippe and Gaston, who both went into the business. When Charles Frederick died in 1895, Gaston took on the administration and Jean-Philippe took over the design. In 1952, Maurice and Roger, the fourth generation of Worths to design and administer the house, finally sold out to Paquin, ending the reign of the longest living house in couture.

The tailored suit for women

The Creeds (couture)

Henry Creed is famous for introducing the tailored suit to women, an item he supplied to all the crowned heads of Europe and all the most fashionable women of the day, including Mata Hari who was reputedly shot in a Creed suit.

Another house with English antecedents, James Creed, the first of a long line of tailors, was born in Leicester and moved to London in 1710 where, by cultivating acquaintances with rich men's valets, he acquired a clientele and set up business. This he passed on to his son James who had inherited his father's gift for tailoring and, as his father's apprentice and later his partner, ran a family business which at first was largely limited to repairs and alterations and was located in the City of London. This James had a son, Henry, who after serving a seven-year apprenticeship with several master tailors outshone the more limited talents of his father and grandfather and, by marrying the daughter of a rich City banker, he was able to set up business in the Strand. Henry's only surviving son, another Henry, not only served as apprentice to his now prosperous father who by then had a considerable establishment at 33 Conduit Street, but was also educated as a gentleman, an education that included a tour of Europe. Henry junior,

The Princess von Metternich in a black and white Worth creation designed for her *ca.* 1865.

now a cosmopolitan sophisticate, tailored exclusively for men of fashion. The Count d'Orsay, a leader of fashion second only to Beau Brummell in sartorial elegance (see Chapter 4), was his most important client and through this association he acquired not only a glittering clientele but also an introduction to the French aristocracy. The Empress Eugénie ordered a riding habit or *amazone*, and Queen Victoria followed suit. In 1850, persuaded by his contacts with the French nobility to set up business in Paris, he opened an establishment in Place de l'Opéra. These very successful tailoring businesses in London and Paris he ran concurrently. He settled his family in London where his son Henry was born in 1863. Whilst overseeing his Paris house he was shot and badly wounded in the 1871 riots.

The young Henry married a Frenchwoman, Aimée Lautrieu, and his establishment was so successful that it included in its clientele most of the crowned heads of Europe. Henry Creed would travel with a workshop of twenty hands from court to court – Spain, Italy, Russia and Austria. It was this Henry who introduced men's tailoring to women, supposedly when the Duke of Alba ordered a tweed suit for himself and a matching one for the Duchess.

Without the introduction by Henry Creed of menswear tailoring into womenswear we would have no Yves Saint Laurent 'Le Smoking', Giorgio Armani's working woman's suit, or Claude Montana's power suit. Henry's son Charles set up the very successful house of Charles Creed in Basil Street, London, known for its chic women's tailoring (see Appendix I).

New styles for a new century: the extravagant and the classic

Paul Poiret 1879–1944 (couture)

A Frenchman and great fashion innovator at the beginning of the 20th century, Poiret transformed the look of women's clothes by releasing

A tailored suit by Henry Creed for the Queen of Italy, 1913.

women from the strictures of the corset; his often waistless, abstracted form of garment was revolutionary. As assistant to Charles Frederick Worth, he ran into difficulty and, unable to express his own more radical ideas, he set up on his own in 1904 continuing well into the 1930s. Poiret's taste for exotic oriental pattern and silhouette coincided with the advent of Diaghilev's Ballets Russes, and his designs are best known to us through the fashion illustrations of Georges Lepape in the *Gazette du Bon Ton*, the stylish fashion magazine of the time which also featured drawings by Matisse and Dufy.

Edward Molyneux 1894–1974 (couture)

Known as 'The Captain' from his World War I rank, Molyneux was British, but Irish by birth. He opened his house in Paris at 14 rue Royal in 1919. His impeccable clothes were known for their understated chic. His influence on fashion between the wars cannot be overestimated; he also had houses in London, Cannes, Monte Carlo and Biarritz. During World War II he moved to London but afterwards returned to Paris where his house survived until the mid 1960s. Later in the decade Yves Saint Laurent did a complete collection based on Molyneux's look and he was reputedly Christian Dior's favourite designer. He was a founder member of the Incorporated Society of London Fashion Designers and resigned in 1947 when his sister Kathleen took over the running of the London house. He died in Monte Carlo.

Three powerful women: Chanel, Vionnet and Schiaparelli

Gabrielle Chanel 1883–1971 (couture)

Chanel was a milliner from provincial France whose own charismatic lifestyle and innovative ideas changed fashion thinking. She came to Paris in 1913 and worked as a millinery assistant, and then set up on her own a year later. Her easy informal clothes, her introduction of the sweater, the cardigan, slacks and costume jewellery, now all part of the fashion vocabulary, changed what women wore. The translation of informal menswear items into women's fashion was a revelation.

Using new techniques of making with an emphasis on *fit* – and this meant easy fit – new use of everyday fabrics such as cotton jersey and cotton *drill*, a whole generation of 'chic' French women transformed their look. Her racy lifestyle helped to sell her image and smart women throughout the world wore her scent, Chanel No. 5, if they could not afford to wear her clothes.

Chanel's comeback

In 1955 Gabrielle Chanel reinvented herself, and it was at this point that the Chanel suit, that standby of the fashion repertoire, really came into being. She boldly experimented with new fabrics, especially the knobbly, textured Scottish tweeds from Bernat Klein and Linton Tweeds from Carlisle, with their coarse yarns and vibrant colour combinations. This, together with the technique of *binding* the edges of jackets with wool braid instead of *facing*, and a particularly supple form of make, brought a new life to Chanel tailoring.

At a special showing modelled by her close friends, the Princess de Croy, Marie-Hélène Arnaud (her model protégé), and several others, she launched a look that sent the fashion press wild. The 'Chanel suit ' was copied everywhere. Jeffrey Wallis, a London coat and suit manufacturer and retailer, bought rights to have licensed copies produced which were sold in his own retail outlets, Wallis Shops. Her second incarnation meant that she became once again one of the high priestesses of fashion and her now mature but striking good looks and inimitable chic made her the darling of photographers and journalists. The scent Chanel No. 5 was given a new boost and her stylish house, boutique and

The Chanel suit from her 'comeback' collection, spring 1954.

showroom in the rue Cambon with its famous mirrored staircase became probably the best-known fashion house in the world.

Chanel's second reincarnation

In 1983 Chanel, this time the house rather than the person, went through a second transformation under the leadership of that other Parisian genius Karl Lagerfeld (see below). After Gabrielle Chanel's death in 1971 the house continued but had really more or less fallen into the doldrums churning out copies of the Chanel suit 'verbatim' for rich and not very stylish customers. Lagerfeld transformed both the look and fortunes of this famous old house to the delight and envy of the established fashion world.

Vionnet 1876–1975 (couture)

Madeleine Vionnet, known to the fashion world as the inventor of the *bias cut*, was born in 1876 in Aubervilliers. She went to Paris at the age of 12 where she found work in a millinery work-room and later as a dressmaker. After this she went to London where she worked as a dress-maker for five years, lodging with a doctor who took in mentally ill patients to board, a situation which the young Madeleine found rather disturbing. She consequently returned to Paris and found work with Callot Soeurs and later, in 1907, as the designer at the important fashion house of Doucet, she experimented with unlined and 'unstructured' dress-making techniques. In 1912, one of Vionnet's most celebrated clients, the actress Lanthelme, persuaded her husband to set up Vionnet on her own. Her first house was in the Rue de Rivoli but she later moved to the Avenue Montaigne where her fluid, unlined bias cut clothes became the strongest influence on fashion-able clothes of the mid 1930s. She famously created these deceptively simple but intri-cately cut garments on the poupée, a doll or miniature dress stand. From these miniature designs, experimental patterns were cut by her premières with Vionnet supervising every detail.

Like the later Madame Grès, Vionnet did not draw her designs but relied on creating them in three dimensions on the stand, and it was up to her personally trained cutters to translate these into working patterns and toiles. These were modified from season to season perfecting form, fit, shape and line as a gradual, ever-developing process. Patterns were stored and filed for future reference.

Surprisingly for a designer who considered the next generation of designers as not proper couturiers, her patterns were sold to American stores at quite an early date, pre-empting in some aspects ready-to-wear methods. Although considered the prime example of haute couture, her faultless garments went into a kind of wholesale production by this process. At this period, Vionnet was dubbed the best dressmaker in the world and her house was immensely successful.

For a time the house was the biggest in Paris, employing a vast number of workers. The welfare of these was of great importance to her and she set up special canteens and medical care units within the house. She closed in 1939 when her soft, fluid style had been overtaken by the hard, structured style of the 1940s.

Elsa Schiaparelli 1890–1973 (couture)

The third powerful design force of the 1930s was Elsa Schiaparelli, an Italian born in Rome and who had originally studied philosophy. In New York she married and had a daughter, but when in 1920 her husband left her, she moved with her daughter to Paris, penniless. She designed a, now famous, trompe l'oeil sweater which was fortunately seen by a fashion buyer who ordered it, and her fashion career took off. Her witty surrealist clothes were, by the mid 1930s, the rage of chic Paris and she opened a couture boutique in the exclusive Place Vendôme in 1935. Her autobiography, called *Shocking Life*, gives an indication of her eccentricities.

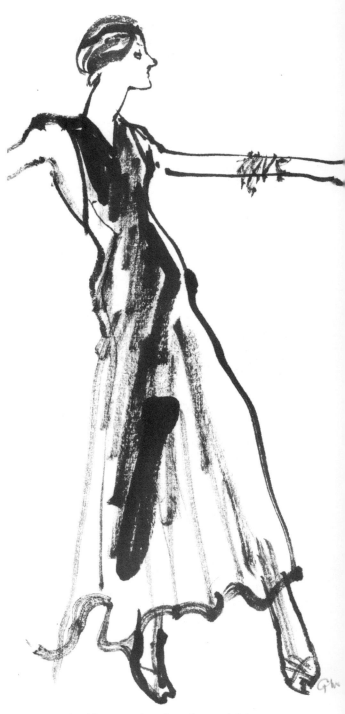

Black crepe backless evening dress by Madeleine Vionnet 1933.

Often working with the surrealist artists such as Salvador Dali, she created clothes that bordered on fine art. Her shoe-hat, her zip-fastener dress, the introduction of a new colour 'shocking pink' and a scent with the same name had an outrageousness that at the time made them the smartest and most desirable items imaginable. Jean Cocteau and Christian Bérard collaborated on her collections. She had buttons in the shape of guitars, animals, masks and padlocks. She invented handbags that were illuminated inside or played a tune like a musical box when they were opened. The square shoulders, conical hats and high hairstyle that typified the 1940s were ideas introduced by her in the late 1930s. Her rival Chanel called her 'the Italian artist who makes dresses'.

Two opposing forces: the New Look and free form

Christian Dior 1905–57 (couture)

Christian Dior is known universally as the creator of the New Look. Born in Granville, his father was the head of an industrial concern. After the early death of his mother in 1932, his father suffered a severe financial setback and Christian had to find work, first as an illustrator with the newspaper *Le Figaro* and later for Robert Piguet as a fashion illustrator. In 1941, however, he was offered a post as modeliste at Lucien Lelong, one of the most respected fashion houses in Paris; Lelong was later to be made president of the Chambre Syndicale de la Couture Parisienne. The other assistant designer at Lelong was another future fashion star, Pierre Balmain. In 1946, Dior met the fabric tycoon Marcel Boussac who set him up as a couturier in his own house in the avenue Montaigne.

In the spring of 1947 Dior showed his first collection, later to be dubbed the New Look. This was a reversal of everything that had gone before: the austerity of the war, square shoulders, angular lines. The New Look was extravagant,

'Daisy', a tailored suit from Christian Dior's New Look collection spring/summer 1947.

ultra feminine, romantic, with a soft sloping shoulder-line, a tiny waist, flowing and voluminous ankle-length skirts and, above all, the spirit of a new, post-war era. The New Look took the fashion world by storm and for fashion journalists it was the only story of the season. It also met with a lot of criticism. Many people, especially politicians, felt its extravagant use of fabric, often as much as 50 metres a dress, was exorbitant and went against the whole idea of post-war economy. It did, however, change fashion; a season later not a single designer was showing a short skirt or a square shoulder. For the next ten years he was the most successful designer in Paris, if not the world. His H, A and Y lines of successive seasons were discussion topics for everyone not just the fashion cognoscenti.

He died in 1957 at the age of 52. He was succeeded in the house by his protégé Yves Saint Laurent, who, after a brilliant but badly received collection, was dismissed in 1960. The house was then taken over by Marc Bohan, subsequently by Gianfranco Ferre in 1989 and in 1996 by John Galliano.

Cristobal Balenciaga 1895–1972 (couture)

Balenciaga was known to his contemporaries as 'the master': his influence on fashion was so great that, for a time, it was difficult to appreciate this quiet revolution. His abstract shapes and style of shaping and cutting had been incorporated into every strata of the fashion industry from high fashion to the mass market. However, at the time of its inception *'free form'*, as it was known, was quite revolutionary. A sculptural shape that hung from the shoulders and was apparently independent of the body was something quite new. It flew in the face of all dressmaking and cutting rules and was at first abhorrent to most fitters and cutters. Poiret may have hinted at the notion but Balenciaga carried it to its ultimate conclusion. He was the antithesis of his fellow couturier Christian Dior. Where

Dior was romantic, pretty, feminine, extravagant and glamorous, Balenciaga was austere, sculptural and almost masculine. Hated by Gabrielle Chanel for eschewing the feminine body shape, he not only influenced a generation of designers but also changed forever the way clothes were constructed. He considered himself a tailor, and the cut of these abstract shapes was immaculate. The Balenciaga 'school' included in its adherents Hubert de Givenchy, André Courrèges, Pierre Cardin and Emanuel Ungaro. In fact these

Balenciaga evening dress and cape in black silk faille, 1953.

125

protégés had been either assistants, tailors or apprentices in his atelier.

The influence of Spain in Paris in the mid 1950s was significant (for example Picasso, Miro and Picabia) and other design houses had taken on Spanish designers, for example Castillo at Lanvin. Balenciaga's clients were almost like disciples and when his house was at its height, it was almost impossible to become a new client without the most complicated introduction, perhaps through a friend, to one of the vendeuses. His clients included the socialite Gloria Guinness, and his clothes were the most expensive in Paris, and that of course meant the world. The super-rich South Americans were some of his most loyal clients. His style was definitely an acquired taste, but a taste popular with European royalty: Queen Fabiola of Belgium was married in a Balenciaga. Wedding dresses had this same inimitable, sculptural quality and attention to detail that made not only his suits but also his ball dresses the envy of the fashionable set. He was for a time the darling of the *grandes dames* of the fashion press such as Carmel Snow, Diana Vreeland and Ernestine Carter.

Somehow these supremely simple but difficult-to-construct shapes filtered down to mass production. Every coat and suit manufacturer re-cut their **blocks** to incorporate the famous Balenciaga **kimono sleeve**, the unfitted waist and the seven-eighths coat length. Evening dress manufacturers constructed free-form, bell-shaped cocktail dresses. Of course, many paid their £1000 to attend the collection in Avenue Georges V and had either toiles or tissue paper replicas to bring home and copy as part of the deal.

Finally, however, this commercialisation of a look that was supremely non-commercial dealt its own deathblow. As is the inevitable way with fashion, the hard, sculptural shapes of one era gave way to the softer shapes of the ready-to-wear designers such as Sonia Rykiel of the next.

The genius of the second half of the 20th century

Yves Saint Laurent b. 1936 (couture, RTW)

The story of Yves Saint Laurent is now part of fashion history. At the age of 18 he won a national dress design competition and, through this, was offered what at the time was the best fashion opportunity in the world, the job of assistant to Christian Dior. Not so well known is that the runner up in the competition was Karl Lagerfeld. Yves' time at Dior, however, was not a happy one. On Christian Dior's death in 1957 Saint Laurent took over the designing at the house of Dior. His first collection there was a great success but a subsequent collection based on 'Blouson Noir' or the French version of bikers in skinny leather, mock crocodile and fur was not at the time understood by the fashion press. Today this collection is considered one of the classics in fashion evolution. It brought a young and irreverent element into high fashion and in some ways was the first example of street fashion being the source of high fashion, a trend later to be followed by Pierre Cardin, André Courrèges and Emanuel Ungaro *et al*.

This criticism by the press, together with his call-up for French National Army service, led to what journalists of the day described as a breakdown and his dismissal. This, of course, was a blessing in disguise as it led to his setting up on his own, a venture that was brave and fraught with danger for a designer so young and relatively inexperienced. He opened the house of Saint Laurent in 1962 at 31 rue Spontini and he was assisted by his brilliant business manager Paul Bergé. This partnership, which lasted until 2002, may be the key to the gigantic success of the house of Saint Laurent. Eventually Yves Saint Laurent became the darling of the fashion press, largely, it has been claimed, owing to the influence of John Fairchild of *Women's Wear Daily*.

Safari outfit by Yves Saint Laurent
from the spring/summer 1968
collection.

Saint Laurent was the first of the great couturiers to exploit the power of ready-to-wear, setting up YSL Rive Gauche in 1966 and his menswear division in 1974. His fashion innovations include 'Le Smoking', the trouser suit, the see-through top, cross-dressing, ethnic peasant- and African-inspired clothes and unisex fashion.

Many would proclaim Yves Saint Laurent the greatest fashion designer of the 20th century and the house is still powerful in the 21st. Saint Laurent showed his last collection in the autumn of 2002 to huge acclaim from the people of Paris. The acquisition of YSL ready-to-wear by Gucci in 2000 and the advent of Tom Ford as creative director of the ready-to-wear collections have added another element to this story.

Casual classicism

Claire McCardell 1905–58 (RTW)

The inventor of the quintessential American look, McCardell created soft, unstructured sportswear – remarkably simple yet brilliantly cut. The cotton wrap skirt, the *dirndl* skirt, the wrap top and the use of wool for evening clothes were all part of a throwaway chic that personified her clothes.

Born in Frederick, Maryland, McCardell was the daughter of a prominent banker and senator. After studying at Parsons School of Design in New York she worked first as a model and then as a designer on the staff of Hattie Carnegie. In 1931 she became assistant designer to Townley Frocks. Here she designed her first collection and on the death of the head designer took over the responsibility for designing and producing the house's collections.

Her 'monastic' dress, the 'popover' wrap dress and her 1946 'baby' dress were instant classics and influenced world fashion. *Time Magazine* praised her 'artist's sense of colour and sculptor's feeling for form' when she was on their cover in 1955.

Jean Muir 1933–95 (RTW)

Muir's emphasis on the craft skills of dressmaking made her London's supreme classic designer. Recognised throughout the world as a fashion leader, she started in London at Liberty's as a saleswoman of lingerie. She later worked for Jaeger and the great hat designer Aage Thaarup. She first made her mark as the designer at Jane and Jane, and later she set up on her own.

Together with Gerald McCann, John Bates and Gina Fratini, Muir was part of London's fashion revival of the 1960s. Her own style, however, was the reverse of the 'London Look': restrained, beautifully cut, in downbeat colours and using only the best and subtlest of fabrics. Her typically sparse, well-ordered workshop was in itself a statement of her intent. She employed a handful of skilful workers, creating the atmosphere of a couturier's atelier rather than the ready-to-wear design workroom that it actually was. Her pale, nearly white complexion and her dark, nearly black lipstick together with her black, bobbed hair and her clipped way of speaking made her a fashion icon recognised throughout the world.

Sonia Rykiel b. 1930 (RTW)

In 1962, Sonia Rykiel, unable to find any soft sweaters during her pregnancy, knitted her own and then began selling them in her husband's fashion shops. The knitted sweater became her symbol and the Americans crowned her 'Queen of Knits'. She was one of the key figures in the rising importance of the ready-to-wear créateurs. With her sweater dress, cardigan, knitted two-piece and her trademark – overlocked seams visible on the outside of the garment – she was, in many ways, the natural successor to Chanel. This easy 'garçonne' approach to fashion had for several years such an effect on French fashion that her sales amongst Frenchwomen topped those of all her rivals. She calls her clothes 'le nouveau classicisme'.

Since opening her first shop in Galeries Lafayette in 1968, she has expanded her empire to include a chain of boutiques. In the mid 1980s she was vice-president of the Chambre Syndicale.

New York style

Norman Norell 1900–72 (couture)

Norman Norell was to American fashion what Balenciaga was to Paris couture: the master, often called 'the dean of American fashion designers'. The simple, clean-cut, classic look which typifies American fashion and was later taken up by Halston, Calvin Klein and Donna Karan has its very obvious roots in Norell's simply cut coats and suits and sleek but glamorous evening dresses. Considered as one of the few American couturiers, in fact he is said to be 'among the first to employ couture techniques and provide couture quality in ready-made clothing' – a clear indication of the difference between European and American couture.

Born in 1900, Norman Levinson changed his name to Norell when he came to New York, taking the 'Nor' from Norman and 'ell' from the first letter of Levinson. He studied fashion illustration at the famous Parson School of Design and later joined the staff at Hattie Carnegie where he designed and adapted Paris models for such celebrities as Gertrude Lawrence, Paulette Goddard and Ina Claire.

In 1941 he teamed up with the manufacturer Anthony Traina to become for a period Traina-Norell. Feted by the American fashion press, he won most of their coveted awards and was founder and first president of the Council of Fashion Designers of America.

Mainbocher 1890–1976 (couture)

Mainbocher, whose real name was Main Rousseau Bocher, was the first American to open a couture house in Paris. His simple, elegant clothes were comparable to those of Molyneux.

Cream whipcord coat from Norman Norell 1950.

Just by using stripes or spots he was able to create a stylish silhouette. He was a great favourite of Wallis Simpson and designed her wedding dress when she married the Duke of Windsor in 1937. Earlier in his career he was a successful fashion journalist in both New York and Paris and became editor of *French Vogue*. He had the ability to foresee the next fashion movement – just before World War II, when everything was long and narrow, he introduced full-skirted ball dresses. He moved his house to New York at the outbreak of the war and ran a successful business until not long before he died.

The Sixties

Mary Quant b. 1934 (RTW)

In the late 1950s, young fashion was to be found in a boutique in the King's Road, Chelsea, called Bazaar. This was owned by a young designer called Mary Quant and her business manager husband Alexander Plunket Greene. Quant, together with the now forgotten Kiki Byrne, then represented the only real alternative, at high fashion level, to the haute couture designers whose designs at that time were sophisticated but certainly not young.

Quant was trained at Goldsmith's School of Art in London. She, like Courrèges and Cardin, foresaw the youth revolution of the 1960s. She stocked and later designed and produced young fashion at affordable prices. Quant, together with Courrèges, is considered the inventor of the mini skirt. Her influence on young fashion was immense and the great changes in British fashion are largely due to her innovations. From these small beginnings she built up a huge fashion empire, designing everything from cosmetics to bed linen. Her minimal mini dress will remain a symbol of the Swinging Sixties.

Mary Quant wears Mary Quant, late 1960.

André Courrèges b. 1923 (couture)

Born in Pau, France, Courrèges is considered together with Mary Quant as the inventor of the mini skirt. His training at Balenciaga as a cutter meant that he not only developed designing skills but also became a master tailor. In 1961 he set up independently with his wife and just two workers at 48 avenue Kléber but by 1965 he had 54 people working for him. His breakthrough came with his space-age collection which stunned the fashion press with its clean, structured cut, use of white, the 'mini jupe', white ankle boots and white-framed dark glasses. His designs were copied throughout the world and his influence on fashion was great but short-lived. The brand continues today.

Pierre Cardin b. 1922 (couture)

Pierre Cardin's roots, like those of Courrèges, are also in tailoring. He worked at Paquin where he collaborated with Antonio Castillo (later of Lanvin Castillo) on the costumes for Jean Cocteau's famous film *La Belle et la Bête*. He presented his first haute couture collection in 1953 at 118 rue du Faubourg Saint Honoré. In 1960 he was one of the few Paris designers to incorporate the ideas of the 1960s fashion revolution into both his womenswear and menswear designs. This was a new departure for designers. A brilliant publicist and innovator, he is, like Courrèges, dubbed a space-age designer. He is a creative genius with unstoppable energy and verve.

Biba – Barbara Hulanicki b. 1938 (RTW)

Barbara Hulanicki, a Polish girl from Brighton, who studied fashion at the art school there, started her career as a highly successful fashion illustrator. Her fashion drawing influenced a generation of British fashion students.

In 1963 she opened a small shop in the back streets of Kensington in London where she sold fashionable young clothes at the prices that the young could afford. This was so successful that she opened a much larger shop in nearby Kensington High Street which helped the street to become one of the centres of 'Swinging London'. This shop was called Biba, the name of Hulanicki's younger sister. It sold a range of clothes that at first were very influenced by the French ready-to-wear designer Emmanuelle Khanh, but which developed into a style that became world famous and was exactly what the young fashionable people of the late 1960s to early 1970s required. It could almost be said to be the impetus for 70s style. Her subtle colour range of tea rose, beige, prune, chocolate and black became so important that mass market companies would send their designers to Biba to buy her range of T-shirts on which they would then base their next season's colour range.

The T-shirts themselves, which were sexy, tight fitting, with low-scooped necklines and drawstring necks were a must for every fashion-conscious person. Wide bottomed satin trousers, *point d'esprit*, *ninon* shirts for men and women, romantic dresses in printed lawns, chiffons and crepes together with her inimitable shoes and boots became the uniform of the fashionable, both the young and the not so young. The High Street Kensington shop was enlarged and Biba was one of the first fashion companies to introduce 'lifestyle' merchandise such as wallpaper, soft furnishings and ornaments.

This shop became so successful that Hulaniki bought out the ailing Derry and Toms, a large department store in High Street Kensington (part of what Londoners called the Holy Trinity: Barkers, Derry and Toms, and Pontings). This was a huge undertaking and broadened her merchandise base even further but eventually proved too much, and in 1975 it folded. This was the end of an amazing one-woman empire that changed the whole tone of high street fashion and shopping habits. She has undertaken several ventures since but on a much smaller scale.

Zandra Rhodes b. 1942 (RTW)

Zandra Rhodes studied textile design at the Royal College of Art in the mid 1960s. Her mother had taught dressmaking at Medway College of Art and so fashion was in her blood, but at first she concentrated on textile design and, together with Sylvia Ayton, she set up a shop in Fulham Road, London, called the Fulham Road Clothes Shop.

This shop, although stylistically successful, was not a financial success. After designing textile ranges for companies such as Bellville Sassoon, her appetite for couture and high fashion was awakened and she set up a fashion workshop in Porchester Road, London. Her extravagant colour, brilliant and original prints and amazing abstract shapes gained her a lot of good fashion publicity and her fashion shows at such venues as the Round House, north London, and the Essoldo Cinema in the King's Road, Chelsea, were for a time the fashion events of the year. She had the ability to take the hippie culture with its shock tactics, iconoclastic colour mixes and clothing items (for example the caftan) into high fashion – no pop star's girlfriend was without a Zandra Rhodes. This wild style was slightly tamed by the clever sales direction of Anne Knight, an ex Fortnum and Masons buyer.

In 2003, Rhodes opened her Fashion and Textile Museum in London.

Ossie Clark 1942–96 (RTW)

Rhodes' contemporary at the Royal College of Art and great rival Ossie Clark, whose real name was Raymond, left the Royal College fashion school in 1966 with a spectacular final show – his floor-length transparent plastic raincoat, illuminated with multi-coloured electric light bulbs, was the *pièce de résistance*.

Part of Clark's talent was his ability to transform ideas from the past and make them thoroughly of the moment. However, it was not just as a sensational designer that he really made his name; it was also as a brilliant cutter, maker and flatterer of women that he changed British, and consequently world, fashion for a time. Working with the print designer later to be his wife, Celia Birtwell, he ingeniously worked with crepe, chiffon, satin and even snakeskin to create delectable garments. His immaculate tailoring and masterful cut put him amongst the most influential of all British designers.

His fashion shows at Chelsea Town Hall drew pop stars and the first supermodels; the Rolling Stones and the Beatles rubbed shoulders with aristocracy and the art world. For an outsider, however, entry was impossible. A stormy but highly amusing personality, he numbered the great painters David Hockney and Patrick Proctor amongst his friends.

Clark was part of the ready-to-wear revolution; his make, fabric choice, price range and availability had nothing to do with haute couture, but his innovation, style and verve were of the highest quality.

Drawing from Ossie Clark's sketchbook *ca.* 1970.

Left: Crinoline in printed chiffon from Zandra Rhodes' 1973 collection. (Photograph by Jo Gaffney.)

133

New couture

Karl Lagerfeld b. 1938 (couture and RTW)

The first sign of haute couture's renaissance was in 1983 when Karl Lagerfeld took over as artistic director of the ailing house of Chanel and showed the fashion world the way forward.

Lagerfeld, born in Hamburg of German/Swedish parentage, went to Paris at the age of 14, and at 16 was the runner-up to Yves Saint Laurent in the prestigious International Wool Secretariat dress design competition. He first found work with the established designer Pierre Balmain, but by 1960 he was a freelance designer for many well-known ready-to-wear companies and a founding member of the newly emerging créateurs. He made his mark as designer for Chloé and was hailed as a genius by the fashion press. One of the most prolific designers in the world, at one time he was designing more collections a year than anyone else, for Chloé, his own label, Krizia, Ballantyne and Fendi furs.

His appointment as artistic director of the house of Chanel in 1983 was a revelation for the fashion industry. Using the inspiration, style and, almost more importantly, the items of the Chanel look – the unlined suit, the frilly debutante short evening dress, the pussy cat bow, the forward tilting hat, the Chanel bag, the gold chain, the strappy sandals and the oversized costume jewellery – Lagerfeld reinvented the look making it entirely up-to-date, surprisingly innovative and highly saleable: a phenomenon that other houses were not slow to appreciate and emulate.

Christian Lacroix b. 1951 (couture)

On 26 July 1987 Christian Lacroix launched the first new couture house to be opened in Paris for twenty-five years, at 73 rue du Faubourg Saint Honoré. Not since 1962, when Yves Saint Laurent opened his house in the Rue Spontini,

Christian Lacroix short evening dress from the haute couture autumn/winter 2001 collection.

had a Parisian designer dared to take this apparently risky step. Lacroix was, however, already a very experienced couture designer having previously been the designer at Jean Patou, and his financial backers were convinced that the time was right to launch another couture house.

Born in Arles, Lacroix studied art history at the University of Montpellier and later at both the Sorbonne and Ecole du Louvre with the intention of becoming a museum curator. Encouraged by friends, he took up designing and found work at Hermès and later at Guy Paulin. In 1981 he became the couture designer to Jean Patou where he rejuvenated the world famous house and in five years had trebled its orders. He designed his last collection for Patou in January 1987.

The house of Lacroix is now well established and has made its mark on the world stage. The Lacroix look is eclectic, colourful, feminine and glamorous and relies on a mixture of colourful prints, embroidery and skilful draping. Lacroix says, 'I want to get back to the position where the couture becomes a kind of laboratory for ideas, the way it was with Schiaparelli forty years ago.' He acquired two very experienced premiers de l'atelier, the tailor came to him from Yves Saint Laurent and from the Viscomtesse de Ribes and the flou (soft dressmaker) had worked for Jacques Fath, Lanvin and Balmain. Lacroix also produces a ready-to-wear collection and a scent.

The renegades: James, Gaultier and Westwood

Charles James 1906–78 (couture)

James was an American fashion renegade who died in poverty but whose influence on other designers was huge. A designer's designer he was born in England in 1906, the son of a British Army officer. The family moved to Chicago where Charles started designing hats at the age of 19 and opened a shop called Charles Boucheron. He subsequently set up couture establishments in London and Paris. In 1930 he set up at 1 Bruton Street in London's Mayfair – he went bankrupt almost immediately and went to Paris to learn 'line, fabric and construction'. Back in London he started evolving designs such as his 'Taxi' dress – this method of evolving rather than designing was peculiar to James. He was described as one who 'designs with a length of fabric and a pair of shears. ... He literally

builds the frock and draws the design after it is finished.' Finally he moved back to New York where he set up a one-man couture business creating, cutting and sometimes even making the garments himself. On the whole these were individual creations for rich women who had to put up with his volatile temperament and often a long wait to acquire these extremely individual works of art. His attempts to enter the ready-to-wear market came to nothing. For a time the designer Halston was his assistant.

The 'Petal' dress, the 'Four-leaf Clover' dress and the 'Padded Jacket' have now become icons of design history but did not earn him a living. In his last years he worked, lived and died at the famous Chelsea Hotel in New York.

Charles James's famous 'Four-leaf Clover' dress originally designed for Mrs William Randolph Hearst Jr in 1953.

135

Jean-Paul Gaultier b. 1952 (couture and RTW)

Born in France, Gaultier worked for Cardin, Esterel and Patou where he was assistant first to Michel Goma and then to Angelo Tarlazzi. Later, as a freelance designer, he came into contact with London's street fashion, which particularly influenced his attitude and work. His genius, however, is in being able to convert apparently outrageous ideas into high fashion. A wicked, sexy sense of humour makes his collections the most memorable and most eagerly awaited of the season. His first collections were ready-to-wear but by 1997 he had moved into couture, showing both menswear and womenswear. His collections are always provocatively named: 'Dadaiste' for the corset dress collection in 1983, 'Homage to Frida Kahlo' and the 'Existentialists' in 1998. He has been dubbed the *enfant terrible* of the French fashion world.

Vivienne Westwood b. 1941 (RTW)

Vivienne Westwood is the wild card of the fashion designer pack. Always a renegade from her first shop in World's End at the then seedy end of the King's Road, London, she has constantly set out to shock but was recognised in the early 1970s as a major world player in the fashion game, especially in America.

Born Vivienne Swires in Tintwistle, Cheshire, Westwood's association with Malcolm McClaren (formerly Edwards) was the starting point of her fashion career with the opening in 1974 of Let It Rock at Paradise Garage at 430 King's Road, an address that would have many aliases over the years: Too Fast to Live Too Young to Die, SEX, Seditionaries and World's End.

The paradox in Westwood's design psychology is her love of classic tailoring and her aspirations towards French haute couture. She is now the only British designer using her own name who is a member of the Chambre Syndicale de la Couture Parisienne and is recognised by Yves Saint Laurent and Azzedine Alaia as a major fashion innovator. The often crazy names of her collections such as 'Pirates', 'Mini Crin' and 'Storm in a Teacup' have gone down in fashion history.

Italian high life and glamour

A peculiarity of Italian alta moda (haute couture) is that so many of its designers come from the Italian nobility: Princess Galitzine, Duchessa Simonetta (di Cesaro), Marchese Pucci (di Barsento) and Princess Giovanna Caracciolo known as **Carosa**. Irene **Galitzine**, born in Tiflis in 1900 and from a Russian family, worked for the Fontana sisters as a model before opening her own house in 1959. Her 'Palazzo Pyjamas' were the rage of 1960 especially with American clients. Also working from Rome, **Simonetta**, born in 1922 of Italian and Russian parentage, and her husband Alberto **Fabiani**, who had a separate, rival house also in Rome, were so successful that they decided to open a joint venture in Paris called Simonetta et Fabiani in 1961. Emilio **Pucci**, born in Naples in 1914, probably did more to introduce Italian fashion to the international market than anyone else. In the 1950s and 1960s his printed, silk, jersey shift dresses were indispensable to the well-dressed woman and his particular take on sportswear influenced the world.

The **Sorelle Fontana**, who were of such influence on Italian couture, were not from this background. Their mother was a dressmaker from Parma whose business the three sisters, Zoe, Micol and Giovanna, took over. In 1936 they moved to Rome and by 1951 their glamorous evening dresses (a particular feature of Italian haute couture) were attracting an international market. They designed costumes for Hollywood films – Elizabeth Taylor, Linda Christian, Ava Gardner, Kim Novak and Audrey Hepburn were all dressed by the sisters. They were founder

Vivienne Westwood's ball dress from her autumn/winter 1998 collection.

members of the Camera Nazionale dell'Alta Moda Italiana, organised by Giovanni Battista Giorgini (see Appendix III).

Roberto **Capucci**, the most inventive of all the Italian couturiers, opened a tiny salon in Florence in 1950 when he was only 21. Highly experimental and always trying to push the boundaries of fashion, his ball gowns of the 1950s were legendary. His place in the history of fashion is alongside Charles James and Cristobal Balenciaga.

Italian couture today

The Camera dell'Alta Moda makes sure that Italian couture still flourishes today: from its base in Rome it arranges up to thirty-one showings per season. Well-known names such as **Lancetti**, **Renato Balestra** and **Rocco Barocco**, together with many new and less well known designers, show in January and July in Rome over several days. World famous names like Valentino and Versace are *membres correspondants* of the Chambre Syndicale de la Couture Parisienne and also show there.

Two short evening dresses by Roberto Capucci, from 1956.

Valentino b. 1932 (couture)

Valentino, whose full name is Valentino Garavani, is the darling of the world's most glamorous women. He was trained at the Chambre Syndicale school and worked for the French designers Jean Dessès and Guy Laroche before setting up his own house in Rome in 1959. Glamour is still the byword for Valentino's designs, the glamour of Hollywood in its prime.

Gianni Versace 1946–97 (couture)

Versace was born in Calabria, the son of a dressmaker. He was a world-class designer whose verve and exuberance, almost verging on the brash, permeated every aspect of his work. His use of scintillating colours and fabrics, the rethinking of the Hermès scarf theme in print ideas and a truly inventive sense of design made his work a favourite of Diana, Princess of Wales. Since his murder in 1997, his sister Donnatella has taken over the house and many film stars wear Versace dresses.

A new tailoring

Giorgio Armani b. 1934 (RTW)

Armani started his career as a window dresser and later as a stylist for Rinascente, Italy's only large department store. Later he became menswear designer to Cerruti. He set up on his own in 1975 with Sergio Galeotti and said, 'I wanted women to be able to wear jackets, like men, without losing anything of their feminine allure'. In the 1980s he was the darling of the career woman, giving her not only power dressing but a subtle and beautifully tailored version of this genre: 'All my work has developed around the jacket … My small crucial discovery lies in having imagined a garment which falls over the body in a surprisingly natural manner.' He transformed tailoring by doing away with heavy interlinings, redrafting the revers and giving both men and women very high quality ready-to-wear, soft-tailored clothes that meant many rich clients abandoned their made-to-measure tailors altogether. His innovations in both men's and women's tailoring have influenced design since the early 1980s.

The Italian ready-to-wear designers

Walter Albini 1941–83

Having worked for some years in Paris as a fashion illustrator, in 1960 Albini returned to Italy to work for Krizia and Basile as a freelance designer. He had a huge influence on 1970s design with a sharp but romantic look – probably the first high fashion designer to show platform soled shoes in his collection.

Dolce b. 1958 and Gabbana b. 1962

Domenico Dolce from Palermo and Stefano Gabbana from Milan, famous for their extravagant and slightly quirky clothes and their love of black and white and leopard skin, have influenced the high street with a gamut of looks.

Striped woman's suit from Giorgio Armani, September 1995.

139

Romeo Gigli with an outfit from his 1990 collection.

Romeo Gigli b. 1949

After a season in New York with Pietro Dimitri, Gigli returned to Italy to design freelance for Timmi and others. He started his own company in 1983. His rich colours and soft but innovative cut have earned him an international reputation.

Gucci (established 1933)

This now giant Florence-based company was founded by Guccio Gucci who designed the iconic Gucci loafer in 1932 for his saddlery, bag and shoe company. His son Aldo introduced the brand logo, the interlocking Gs of his father's initials. With the introduction of **Tom Ford** as creative director in 1994 the company has taken on a fashion persona of world importance. In 2000 it bought out the once all-powerful Yves Saint Laurent ready-to-wear, putting Ford in charge of design, and in 2001 acquired the names of Alexander McQueen and Stella McCartney.

Missoni, Tai (Ottavio) b. 1921 and Rosita b. 1931

This husband and wife team, that design for and run the hugely successful knitwear company Missoni, met in England after World War II. Tai designs the knit patterns and Rosita designs the shapes. Their inimitable colour story and simple shapes have made the Missoni product a classic. In 1997 the business was taken over by their daughter, Angela.

Moschino 1950–94

Franco Moschino worked first as an illustrator for Gianni Versace and then as a designer for Cadette and Matti. He showed his first collection in 1983. An iconoclastic designer, full of tongue-in-cheek ideas, his humorous and chic clothes were very much in the vein of his compatriot Elsa Schiaparelli. Like her, he achieved worldwide fame.

Miuccia Prada b. 1951

In 1978, Miuccia Prada took over the luxury luggage company founded by her grandfather. With her design talent and the business expertise of her husband Patrizio Bertelli, the business was converted into a multi-million pound ultra high fashion company with the ability to buy out Jil Sander, Helmut Lang and even the long established British shoe company Church and Co.

The impact of the Japanese

The huge impact of the Japanese designers is discussed in depth in Chapter 2 and listed below are thumbnail biographies of the most important.

Rei Kawakubo b. 1942 (RTW) and Yohji Yamamoto b. 1943 (RTW)

Kawabuko of Commes des Garçons was born in Tokyo, and Yamamoto in Yokohama. Both should be credited with the non-cut cutting of the 1980s – setting aside conventional make and symmetry, their innovative and often shocking collections have had a lasting influence on western fashion.

Kenzo b. 1940 (RTW)

Kenzo Takada, born in Kyoto, came to London and Paris in the 1960s, at first producing freelance knitwear collections. By 1970 he was able to set up a shop in Place des Victoires in Paris called Jungle Jap. Simple shapes, exotic prints and a wonderful colour palette have meant the continued success of this label.

Issey Miyake b. 1935 (RTW)

Born in Hiroshima, Miyake went to Paris to study fashion at the Chambre Syndicale School. After working as assistant designer to Guy Laroche and Givenchy he set up a ready-to-wear company which, although highly professional, produced none of the surprises of his later career. Now he is known for avant-garde, highly original shapes and intricate and innovative fabric manipulation.

Kansai Yamamoto b. 1944 (RTW)

Born in Yokohama, Yamamoto went to London where he opened a small fashion shop in the Fulham Road. His ethnic style was just right for the time, the early 1970s, and was often based on traditional Japanese items but exaggerated to the degree where they became high fashion. He moved to Paris in 1975 where his success has continued.

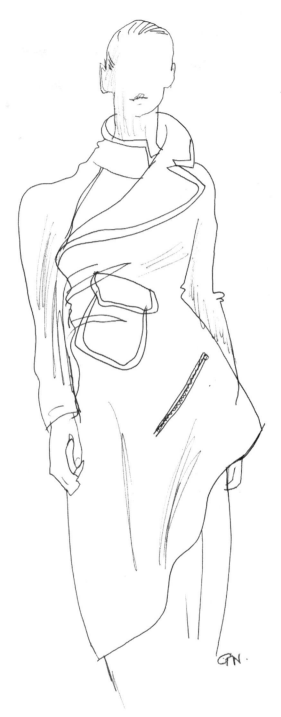

Commes des Garçons – Rei Kawakubo – from the autumn/winter 2002 collection.

The Belgian force

A new force hit European fashion when the 'Antwerp Six' had their first showing in London in 1986. These six, which included Ann Demeulemeester, Martin Margiela and Dries Van Noten, had all studied at the Royal Academy of Arts Antwerp, now the Flanders Fashion Institute (FFI).

Dirk Bikkembergs b. 1959 (RTW)

Bikkembergs graduated in 1982. His first collections were as a shoe designer. In 1987 he launched his first menswear collection. He has gone from strength to strength, often working with Italian production companies. Mostly known for his menswear, he shows in Milan.

Ann Demeulemeester b. 1954 (RTW)

Demeulemeester is probably the best known and most copied of the six. A clean, asymmetrical cut, impeccably tailored and often in black leather, is her hallmark. A neo-rock collection put her firmly on the Paris map and established her as a directional designer.

Martin Margiela b. 1957 (RTW)

From 1984 to 1987, Margiela was design assistant to Jean-Paul Gaultier. He founded Maison Margiela with Jenny Meirs in Paris in 1989. Famous for his deconstruct collections, reassembled garments in recycled fabrics or sweaters made from socks, this almost fine art approach to fashion has proved very successful.

Josephus Thimister b. 1962 (RTW)

Thimister worked for Balenciaga's ready-to-wear house from 1992 to 1997 using details from the archive of the couture house. Now working under his own label, he describes his clothes as 'light, fabric and shadow'.

Dries Van Noten b. 1958 (RTW)

Born to a family of tailors, Van Noten worked freelance for Belgian and Italian labels whilst still a student. In 1991 he launched his first Paris show followed in 1993 by the joint openings of his Paris and Milan showrooms. Van Noten employs a staff of 60 based in Antwerp with a press office in Paris.

Shirt, waistcoat and trousers from Dries Van Noten's spring/summer 2003 collection shown in Paris at the Allée des Cygnes in 2002.

American simplicity

An economy of line and simplicity of cut combined with the sense of supreme wearability characterise the American look. Designers like Ralph Lauren, Calvin Klein, Donna Karan, Michael Kors and Marc Jacobs are the designers of today that epitomise this look.

Marc Jacobs b. 1963 (RTW)

Jacobs is similar in many ways to Kors (see below) and is likewise the design director of a French company, Louis Vuitton.

Donna Karan b. 1948 (RTW)

Karan, whose real name is Donna Faske, comes from the Ann Klein stable. She knows only too well how to convert current looks into easy-to-wear, simple pieces in blacks, greys, browns and taupes. Donna Karan, DKNY, DKNY Jeans, DKNY Men and DKNY Jeans Juniors carry her dressing philosophy to all levels.

Calvin Klein b. 1942 (RTW)

Klein is a minimalist whose simple lines and pared-down colour combinations – he uses black, white and grey to huge advantage – have had a huge influence on all commercial fashion. His success in menswear is equal to that in womenswear where his jeans and men's underwear are world famous.

Michael Kors b. 1959 (RTW)

Kors is another minimalist with American sportswear overtones. This, translated into luxury fabrics in neutrals and brights, gave him the publicity that led to his being employed by the French house of Céline.

Ralph Lauren b. 1939 (RTW)

Lauren, who started making ties for clients when he worked at Brooks Brothers, built an empire first with Polo sportswear and later with a series of collections, both menswear and womenswear, of 'borrowed' classics, outdoing the British at their own game. His lifestyle emporium in New York is practically the re-creation of a Scottish baronial castle.

An Austrian and German duo

Germany, although the largest manufacturer of fashion clothing in Europe, is not known for its high fashion or its original designers with the exception of two innovators, Jil Sander and Helmut Lang.

Helmut Lang b. 1956 (RTW)

Lang is the minimalist of minimalists whose innovative use of man-made fabrics influenced many other designers. The abstract qualities of his designs are not unlike those of the Japanese.

Jil Sander b. 1943 (RTW)

Sander, whose impeccable, simple, almost oriental pieces using a scintillating pastel palette and the highest quality fabrics, became so popular that she was not only able to open a shop in the avenue Montaigne at the centre of Parisian luxury, but also bought out by Prada.

All change

A feature of the big French houses over the past few seasons has been their changes in personnel. Names usually associated with one house are now at another, with the exception of the real French contingent like Gaultier, Lacroix and

Balenciaga (where Ghesquière is still in charge). The English Galliano was at Givenchy but is now at Dior, whilst Julien McDonald (also English) replaced Alexander McQueen who was at Givenchy directly after Galliano. Belgian Martin Margiela is at Hermès, American Marc Jacobs is at Vuitton, fellow American Michael Kors is at Céline, the English Pheobe Philo, replacing another English designer, Stella McCartney, is at Chloé, Alber Elbaz is at Lanvin and Laurent Mercier has taken over from the veteran American designer Oscar de la Renta at Pierre Balmain. Other designers include Risto Bimbiloski, Venera Arapu, Dice Kayek, Fatima Lopes, Maria Grachvogel and Karim Tassi.

It may be too early to put the stars of the moment into an historical context: the heady careers of John Galliano, Alexander McQueen and Tom Ford have yet to have the light of retrospect shone upon them. **John Galliano (couture)**, born in 1960, is perhaps the most experienced of the three, leaving St Martin's School of Art in 1984. He set up his own company straight away to huge acclaim by the press;

his originality and creativity were never in doubt. In 1996, in a bid to bring the kind of pizzazz that Lagerfeld had brought to Chanel and Gaultier had in his own right, the giant conglomerate Moët Hennessy Louis Vuitton (LVMH), which owns Givenchy and Dior, first installed him as designer at Givenchy and later in the same year at Dior. **Alexander McQueen (couture)**, born in 1969, with a similar background, graduated from St Martin's in 1992. His iconoclastic and somewhat brutal approach to fashion would not, on the surface, have made him the ideal choice to take over from Galliano at Givenchy, a house which under Hubert de Givenchy had produced a quintessentially pure type of design – he was the favourite designer for Audrey Hepburn. This, however, is exactly what LVMH wanted, and for several seasons was an extremely successful enterprise. McQueen has now been bought out by Gucci, as has Stella McCartney. Born in 1962, **Tom Ford (RTW)** as creative director of Gucci has also now taken over as artistic director at Yves Saint Laurent Rive Gauche.

Chapter 9
Distribution

Distribution – Buying and selecting – Marketing – Merchandising – Advertising – Display – Selling strategies – Corporate management – Mail order – Department stores – Other retail outlets

Late 18th century illustrations of Paris boutique shop fronts.

Distribution

This rather unromantic term covers the whole process whereby the goods get to the customer. In fashion this means buying or *selecting* the items from the designer or design company and selling or distributing them to the public; in other words this is the transition from wholesale to retail. This process in itself incorporates several sub-processes: *marketing*, *merchandising*, *advertising* and *display*.

Buying and selecting

Traditionally, in both ready-to-wear and mass production, samples or prototypes are presented to the store or retail buyers at catwalk shows, showroom presentations, on stands at fashion fairs, through agents travelling around the country, or by selling direct to known retailers. At the lower end of the market, buyers tend to buy at trade fairs such as Prêt-à-Porter in Paris rather than the designer shows, says Lorraine Harper, former buying director of River Island.

By any of these methods the buyers are able to view, select and place orders across several sizes and colourways from a collection of samples. Only those samples that receive a viable number of orders will then go into production and be ready at the beginning of next season to go into the shop or retail outlet at the appropriate time. Autumn/winter styles are ordered in the previous March, and spring/summer styles are ordered in the previous September.

The top store buyers are all-powerful, wielding that power through the authority given them by the millions of dollars entrusted to them by their stores. They can command front seats at all important fashion shows, together with celebrities and the press, as their presence can put the seal of approval on a newly formed enterprise. With the fashion press scrutinising their reactions and noting their orders, the reactions of these buyers are crucial to a house's success. It was the Americans who set the pattern in this trend – always ahead in marketing, selecting, merchandising and promotional techniques.

The buyers act as the intermediary between the customer and the designer – it is the buyer who selects for his or her customer. This buyer may represent one of the huge American department stores such as Bergdorf Goodman of New York or Neiman Marcus of Dallas, or a small 'madam shop' in a provincial town in the north of England. In the fashion industry his or her power can be immense. By selecting a particular item or sample from a designer, the buyer sets in motion a whole sequence of actions and it is this chain of actions that keeps the entire fashion textile industry turning, each segment relying on the other.

Once the sample is selected and orders placed with the guarantee of the *open to buy* (budget) firmly lodged, the designer or the production manager can order the fabric in bulk – previously he/she only had a small sample length of the fabric to make up the sample garment. The textile manufacturer is then able to go into the production of that fabric – without the promise of potential orders being placed against a fabric style, it would be folly to produce it. The same process applies to belts, buttons, trimmings and decorations. Competitive garment manufacturing units can then be set in train presenting copy samples for approval on price and quality. Press editorial and advertising can begin to tell the customer when and where, next season, the item can be purchased. Buyers can, through their promotion, make or break a designer: an established company can have a renaissance, a young designer their first chance or a well-known house can be ruined. It is the sales, the money made, that is the all-important factor in

determining the success of a designer or a fashion house – and it is through the buyer that this is achieved or not.

Some companies that have their own retail outlets, such as Wallis and Marks and Spencer, ostensibly produce only what they need for their own shops. However, these establishments have to have an equivalent stage of selection and still produce many more samples garments than will finally go into production.

With the unquestionable power and expertise of the buyer it might be thought that each design house producing its own, quite large, collection was an unnecessary luxury. However, where buyers have directly styled their own collections or imposed too many constraints on designers, the results have not been remarkably successful. Ironically the principle of market forces does not really apply to fashion unless we look at brands like Nike and Adidas. In fashion it is the surprise element, the raw creativity of the designer, that drives the fashion cycle – the new trends which in turn drive the customer to buy. However, there is a movement towards retailers having their own design studios where the buyer can influence yarn, colour and product development decisions.

Marketing

Marketing is what makes the product sell; it is the strategy of making sure the customer knows about the product – what it is like, how and where to obtain it and at what price. This entails identifying the customer, their habits, needs, income bracket and lifestyle. The design company has to have developed a sophisticated marketing strategy bearing all this in mind. More and more, the need to target particular buying groups and to spot niche markets has become a priority. The ideal target model – a married couple that has a particular brand of motor car and a disposable income of a certain amount – is now perhaps a dated concept in marketing; things have become more fluid and sophisticated and the power of branding stronger.

Merchandising

Merchandising is the tactical allocation and delivery of the merchandise to the appropriate department store or retail outlet in a particular town or area, maximising each item's sale potential. Merchandisers work in close contact with the buyers and often have responsibility for arranging the finance to buy the stock. Some merchandisers double up as buyers, but this can lead to buying stock merely to satisfy merchandise demand. The visual merchandiser is responsible for the display of stock on the shop floor.

Advertising

Through advertising the fashion wholesaler or retailer tells the public about the goods they have on offer via the fashion media – magazines, newspapers, television or posters on billboards. Magazines are the favourite method since they are the most fertile source – there are so many of them and they cover all markets.

The fashion press has methods of disseminating information through either editorial or paid advertising (see Chapter 10). Editorial is free and is where the fashion editor chooses the item either because of its fashion impact or because it illustrates a particular point that the editor wants to make and it goes into the body of the magazine in the editorial section. This is by far the most effective method of advertising especially as the garment is usually photographed by a well-known photographer on a famous model. No form of advertising can compare in value with this. The editor endorses the fashion value of the item to the customer with no whiff of compromise or coercion and usually in the most glamorous way. Paid advertising is where the company 'buys' space in the advertising section of the magazine or newspaper. By its nature, editorial has by far the biggest impact on the buying public and is the most difficult to get. It is the job of the PR guru to try to pull this off.

Endorsement by celebrities is a huge part of any advertising campaign. Not only do these endorsements increase sales but they also provide substantial incomes for those celebrities involved.

Capes and coats selling wholesale in an 1860s advertisement for Peter Robinson of Oxford Street, London.

An interesting example of a contemporary comparison. Left: an outfit being worn by Doris Turner at a Leicestershire wedding. Right: an illustration from the 1917 Peter Robinson's department store advertisement for 'Lolette', an afternoon or semi evening gown in chiffon taffetas trimmed with marabou, which is of course the same dress.

Display

There are several methods of displaying the goods on offer. They can be displayed in the windows of the department store or retail outlet, on the shop floor or at the *point of sale* – this usually means where smaller items are displayed on the counter. Whichever method is used, enticing the customer to buy that item is the goal. The major department stores spend large sums and much time and effort on window displays and many are famous for them. Smaller outlets pay just as much attention to how their image will project into the street – choosing the right garment to represent their latest merchandise and at the same time making the entrance sufficiently inviting that it will entice the customer in. The strategies are an art and the big department stores employ a large specialist staff with responsibility for this aspect of sales.

Selling strategies

In order to keep sales up, both the design companies and the buyers have to excite the customer. This is why many designers bring out entirely new collections each season. Without this stimulus, sales would drop and businesses would have to stop trading. By making last season's styles out of date, next season's sales are promoted. The stimulus has been extended further by some companies producing new lines every four weeks, or in America a seven-season year.

Phasing

In the past few years other strategies have been employed to stimulate sales such as a technique called *phasing* whereby design companies do not let the whole collection come out at once, but deliver it in parts, usually three. This tactic allows the buyer to test the market and gives the designer the opportunity to adapt or redesign items.

The strategy has to be part of a long-term plan: the turnover time for dyeing or re-colouring a print can be relatively short – about three weeks – but the cloth has to be bought a season in advance and therefore is ordered in *greige* or *grey cloth* state, a neutral that can easily be piece-dyed. By this method styles can be adapted as the season progresses. At the beginning of the autumn season the weather may be exceptionally mild, but by the end of that season more 'Christmassy' items may be required.

Clever retail outlets with specialised tie-ups with design teams and quick turnover manufacturers can keep abreast of trends and corner the market. Designers also have to be aware of phasing, as it requires extra design skills.

Lead times

The buzzword of the past few seasons has been lead times. The lead time is the amount of time it takes from when an idea is first seen on a catwalk or celebrity, to when it appears in the high street. In Britain the three contenders for speed in lead times are Zara, H&M and Top Shop. Zara is a Spanish firm that started by making dressing gowns but now has such a sophisticated manufacturing and distribution system that it can have an item on the rail in the shop four weeks after it was seen on the catwalk. H&M (Hennes and Mauritz, formerly known as Hennes), a Swedish company, has for some years been working on reducing lead times employing just-in-time technology. The British Top Shop, bought out in 2002 by Philip Green, is following suit.

In order to meet the schedules that short lead times impose, some companies have brought their production back to Europe from the Far East, although this region remains a popular option together with Turkey and eastern Europe. Zara, a vertical operation, has always had its production in Spain, keeping its designers, factories and distribution centres all on one site. The success of this strategy is proved by the fact that Zara's customers shop there seventeen times a year compared with the usual four times for the other high street stores.

In an interesting move to counter claims of copying, Top Shop has recently employed designers Zandra Rhodes and Hussein Chalayan to develop original ranges exclusively for them.

Corporate management

The career patterns of many middle market fashion companies such as Wallis, Alexon, Warehouse, Principles and Miss Selfridge are as convoluted as any of the individual designers' careers. Usually starting out as a single, successful, individual design company, it is bought out by another company, then another, and then by a large conglomerate. This conglomerate can then sell off its parts, take on new, related companies or be bought out by an even larger multinational company, and the individual identity of the original design company can be lost in the process. Wallis is a good case in point.

In the early 1960s, Jeffrey and Harold Wallis took over the family business founded in the 1930s. It had two lines: coats, overseen by Jeffrey, and dresses by Harold. Its great selling point was its copies of Chanel suits, but like other companies of the time it bought designs from all the great Paris couturiers such as Dior, Saint Laurent and Chanel. An arrangement was made whereby toiles, designs and patterns were bought on the understanding that they would be copied but not produced until after the items had appeared in the press, in other words after the press release date.

Later, Jeffrey and Harold Wallis were farsighted enough to employ Royal College of Art graduates to design original collections, not copies. Sylvia Ayton was brought in to design the coats and suits. She had studied at Walthamstow College of Art and then the Royal College and had been co-owner of the Fulham Road Clothes Shop with Zandra Rhodes, her contemporary at the RCA. Valerie Couldridge, another Royal College graduate, designed the dress range. The success of the enterprise made Wallis Shops, with an outlet in every high street in Britain, the fashion Mecca for the smart woman in the street and demonstrated how young design talent could be harnessed and made commercial.

This commercial success, however, meant that Wallis was targeted by larger companies and was eventually acquired by Sears to become part of its portfolio, which by 1985 included Warehouse, Miss Selfridge and Richard Shops. Jockeying for places in a world market, Sears then sold on, dropping the apparently less successful, smaller or weaker companies, though not Wallis, and was finally bought by Arcadia, the new name of the giant Burton Group (see Chapter 5). Further selling off and buying has meant the grouping and regrouping of many of Britain's best-known high street fashion producers and outlets. Alexon, the British Shoe Company, Top Shop, Warehouse, Richard Shops, Dorothy Perkins, Principles and Eastex have all been involved in this exercise. Smaller companies like Racing Green and the mail order company Hawkeshead have also been taken over. These fashion entrepreneurs of that time, including Philip Green, John Osborne, Ralph Halpern, Derek Lovelock and George Davis, formerly of Next, Asda and now Marks and Spencer, gave a cutting edge and a frisson to the fortunes of these well-known companies. By October 2002, Green had taken over Arcadia.

This phenomenon is by no means just a characteristic of the British fashion marketplace – the European version is even more complicated. At the top end of the market the buy-ups and sell-offs were and are still a major feature of European fashion. The giant Moët Hennessy Louis Vuitton (LVMH) has been changing the face of European fashion over the last decade. Based in Paris, with a turnover of £4.6 billion in 1999, it bought Givenchy, Christian Dior, Céline, Loewe, Christian Lacroix and Kenzo. This company started the trend of consciously employing avant-garde designers: Galliano at Dior and Alexander McQueen at Givenchy; it is rumoured that the couture sections of these houses make huge losses, but the knock-on effect of highly newsworthy designers bring in vast revenues for their ancillary products.

Vuitton, like other giants such as Gucci, owned by Pinault-Printemps-Redoute Plc, and Prada, which is privately owned, all started as high quality leather goods manufacturers. Milan-based Prada owns Helmut Lang, Jil Sander, Church and Co. (the old English shoe-maker) and Police/Fila sunglasses. Gucci, based in Florence, employed American designer Tom Ford to completely change its look and now has a turnover of £690 million. Fifty years ago none of these companies was considered by the fashion cognoscenti as of any importance. In terms of sales, though, by 2000 they had overtaken former giants Chanel, worth £420 million, Armani £500 million, Versace £340 million and Hermès £500 million. Yves Saint Laurent who for so long outstripped all but LVMH has been bought out by Gucci.

Mail order

Another important method of distributing merchandise to the buying public is through mail order. America seems to have been in the vanguard in this method of distributing illustrated price lists or catalogues and delivering, by post, the orders placed by customers against the illustrated items – a system necessary for a vast country with scattered, outlying areas that had no retail outlets of their own. The pioneers in this method of selling were Sears and Roebuck, founded in 1886 and which at first sold only watches, and later, in 1872, Montgomery Ward, who started the world's first merchandising mail order company.

Mail order relied on catalogues and a good postal system, sending out catalogues and later distributing orders to outlying areas such as the Mid West and the corn belt. Chicago was the centre for drapery and clothing, or dry goods as they were called, and Montgomery Ward had joined the leading dry goods company there, Field, Falmer and Leiter (see Couture). This company later became the great department store Marshall Field which was to have such an influence on wholesale fashion. Ward hit on the idea of buying dry goods at a low cost for cash and, by eliminating the middleman in order to cut costs, offering those goods at competitive prices to remote areas. Customers would send him an order by mail and he would arrange for the goods to be delivered to the nearest railroad station. Later, with new business partners, he published the first price list, and they themselves described it as 'the world's first general merchandise catalogue'.

It has been said that the mail order catalogue was perhaps the greatest influence in increasing American middle-class living standards and purchasing power. Clothing was just one part of this giant enterprise, but mail order was probably the only way in which people in outlying areas of America could acquire ready-made garments. Montgomery Ward continued until 1985 and Sears is still flourishing, opening a new shop in Chicago in 2002. Mail order continues to be a successful method of selling at all levels and whatever volume – large or small. In Britain, mail order catalogues and brochures abound, from big firms such as Kay's and Littlewoods to small country town concerns that distribute brochures in the popular magazines. It is still an efficient and convenient way of selling clothing. In the past few years this method of selling has been given a huge boost by the internet.

Department stores

Department stores were set up in the 19th century as a selling space open to all, with a fixed price for goods (see Glossary); the reduction of profit margins was made possible by the huge volume of sales. The soaring of industrial production, aided by the growth in railways, allowed for an abundance and variety in manufactured goods. These factors, together with a huge rise in the urban population, could only lead to success for this method of selling.

Above: the salon for blouses and tea gowns at Harrods, London, at the end of the 19th century.

Below: the front of the world famous Harrods store in the 1920s.

London's exclusive Fortnum and Mason store in Piccadilly.

Above left: the first premises acquired by the cousins Theophile Bader and Alphonse Khan on the corner of the Chaussée d'Antin and Lafayette streets, Paris, later to become Galeries Lafayette. Above right: the interior of Galeries Lafayette today showing the dome.

New York store Bloomingdale's in three guises. Top left: *ca.* 1872 on Third Avenue. Top right: its impressive building in the 1950s. Below: a bustling street scene showing its newly built premises in 1930 on the corner of 59th Street and Lexington Avenue.

Britain, with high quality stores such as Harrods, Liberty, Fortnum and Mason, and Marshall and Snelgrove, has always been associated with the development of the department store, although Aristide Boucicaut is credited with inventing the first genuine department store, Le Bon Marché, in Paris in 1869. His rivals, the cousins Theophile Bader and Alphonse Khan, opened a small fashion store on the corner of Lafayette and Chaussée d'Antin streets which later became the giant Galeries Lafayette. In time, with Au Printemps next door, this section of the Boulevard Haussman became a retail shopper's paradise. America, it could be said, developed the concept to its highest form of sophistication – New York stores Saks of Fifth Avenue and Bloomingdale's have a worldwide reputation – their buyers, together with those from Bergdorf Goodman and I. Magnim, are high on the invitation list of any European designer who wants to compete in the international markets.

The department store is still a major factor in disseminating fashion clothing to the public, although this is perhaps being undermined by the proliferation of shopping centres (these are not dissimilar to department stores with their concession shops). Without the gigantic sales of the department stores, though, it is questionable whether the fashion industry could continue in the way it does.

Other retail outlets

Department stores are only one type of retail outlet. Many small shops that used to be called boutiques, an independent designer shop selling its own label, no longer exist in the form familiar in the 1960s, for example Hung On You or Granny Takes a Trip. Now, because retailing is so high powered, small outlets will usually be a franchise such as a Benetton shop, a branch of a multiple (e.g. Jigsaw), part of an international company (e.g. Gap), the outlet for a vertical company (weaver to wearer; e.g. Wallis), or an independent enterprise that buys in designer ready-to-wear pieces (e.g. Browns of South Molton Street).

Discount factory shops and retail outlet villages account for a surprisingly large percentage of the retail market. In Britain, a good example of a discount store is TK Maxx which buys in discontinued lines, cancelled orders and unsold goods from all levels of producers, from high fashion to the cheapest. Factory outlets are clothing manufacturers that sell direct to the customer from their factory. Markets where clothes are sold by street traders at very reduced prices also deal in ends of lines, seconds and similar discount merchandise. Vintage clothing and designers' samples have moved upmarket and are more likely to be found in specialist shops or alternative markets like that in Camden Town, London.

The Saks of Fifth Avenue (New York) flagship store today.

155

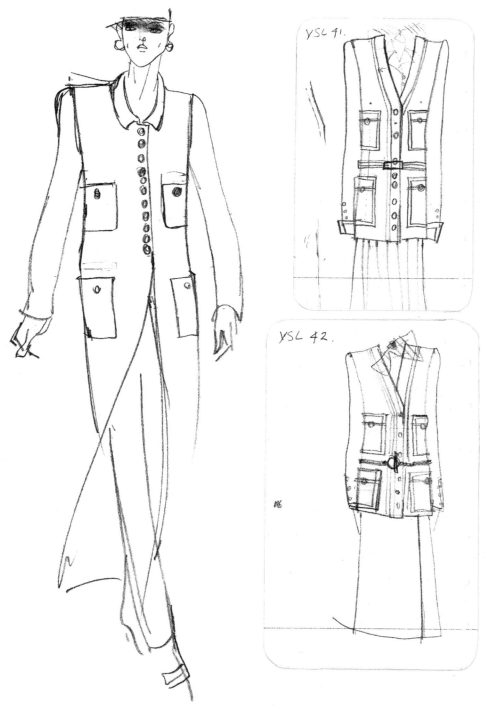

Images from the working sketchbook of Sylvia Ayton, coat and suit designer at Wallis. Left: a long cardigan coat influenced by Chanel. Right: two drawings done at or directly after seeing the Yves Saint Laurent's 'Homage to Chanel's' show in 1972.

Chapter 10
Fashion Organisation and Calendar

The press – Public relations – Fashion forecasting – The fashion stylist –
The fashion educators – Fashion schools – Recruitment agencies – Models and
model agencies – The fashion calendar

The press

The press is the collective word for newspapers, journals, magazines, trade magazines and television, and it is through the fashion press in particular, be it editorial or advertising, that information about a designer, a new look, a fashion house, or a celebrity's latest dress reaches the public and, more importantly, the buying public. Most daily newspapers have a particular day devoted to fashion, for example *The Times* on Tuesday. A whole range of fashion magazines cover a huge market sector, from the exclusive *Vogue* reader to the schoolgirl reading *Dazed and Confused*. Trade magazines such as *Drapers Record* cater for those working in the business, and American publications such as *Bobbin* deal with industrial questions and innovations. A fairly recent phenomenon is the celebrity interest magazine, for example *Hello* and *OK*.

The power of the press

Not so well known in Britain, *Women's Wear Daily* is considered by the fashion industry to be the most powerful journal in the world. Published and edited by the influential John Fairchild, how a collection is received by the journal is said to make or break a company – this is because it can influence the buyers and in turn the great American buying public. Equally influential are the glossy magazines *Vogue*, *Uomo Vogue*, *Harpers*, *Elle*, *The Face*, *i-D* and *Marie Claire*.

The editors

The editors are the all-powerful men and women who direct the teams that produce the articles for the editorial section of a magazine or newspaper. The great commentators, arbiters and critics of fashion have been the clever journalists whose often-cryptic comments so affect what we wear, and their power cannot be over-rated. They include Carmel Snow, Ernestine Carter, Prudence Glynn, Diana Vreeland, Alison Adburgham, Anne Scott-James, Claire Rendelsham and, today, Suzy Menkes, Grace Coddington, Anna Wintour and Hilary Alexander. Some editors, for example Carmel Snow and Diana Vreeland, became *monstres sacrées*, always given the front seat at a show and revered and even feared by some of the designers.

The editor sets the mood and in many cases makes the final choice of what will and what will not go in the magazine. The fashion journalists at newspapers – such as Ernestine Carter on *The Sunday Times*, Prudence Glynn on *The Times*, Alison Adburgham on *The Guardian* and, today, Suzy Menkes on the *Herald Tribune* – were or are brilliant fashion writers and in many cases their words have been the definitive comment on a designer and sometimes on society as a whole. Newspaper fashion journalists working through their assistants, sub-editors and editors find out exactly what is happening. They visit all the designers' shows and showrooms and from these select items, a garment that might go into a feature. The items are then sent to the magazine's or newspaper's headquarters and the team makes a final selection from a rail where all the items are put on view. In the end, of course, only very few items can be selected, but experienced designers are used to this. The theme of the feature is decided upon, models and a photographer are chosen and a photographic shoot arranged with make-up artist and stylist to assist. For a newspaper shoot the results will be seen fairly immediately, but for a glossy magazine several months elapse before publication.

It is the job of the designer's public relations officer or company to get as much press coverage as possible in order to solicit interest in a designer, item or range and to liaise with the newspaper's or magazine's editorial staff. Getting good publicity is not easy as there is so much competition.

Public relations

The public relations (PR) consultant or company is an integral part of the fashion process. Although the fashion press is always on the look-out for new trends and designers, there has to be a liaison between the designer of a fashion company and the press and this is the role of the PR company. There are, of course, other methods of making sure a fashion name is kept in the public eye other than through press coverage, but it is primarily through the press, be it newspapers, magazines, trade journals or advertising, that a fashion name is kept alive.

Press launches are very much part of the PR's repertoire: these are events such as a reception in a smart hotel or up-to-the-minute gallery where the designers can present themselves or their work to the press. The idea is to get as many pieces of editorial coverage from this as possible – editorial in a major newspaper can be worth many thousands in sales.

Fashion forecasting

The background to fashion forecasting

The necessity for fashion forecasting arose out of a need by large wholesale fashion companies and garment manufacturers in the 1960s and 1970s to keep abreast of what was happening and what was likely to happen in an increasingly competitive fashion market. In the past, these companies had relied on copying individual couture, and in particular Paris couture, items and sending their designers to the Paris collections to get ideas and a precise knowledge of what was happening that season. Wholesale houses paid a large fee to go to these shows and in many cases, as part of the fee, could bring home a calico toile or paper replica of the model that they felt best suited their market. Many companies made direct copies and promoted them as such, whereas other companies used their designers to do adaptations.

It was part of the wholesale designer's responsibility to sketch and remember every item they had seen at a show. Company designers could be seen after the shows sitting in cafés furiously drawing as many items as they could remember. Unofficial photography, drawing or making sketches at the shows were strictly forbidden by the couture houses; reports on secret cameras hidden in handbags or umbrellas were a favourite item for the press. The fashion press, both newspapers and magazines, was not allowed to publish photographs until quite a long time after the shows had taken place. This prevented copies being made before the couture customers had taken delivery of their orders and stopped any wholesaler who had bought a toile being forestalled by another company. This lag between showing and publishing was part of the agreement between the press and the Chambre Syndicale in Paris, the Incorporated Society in London and the Camera dell'Alta Moda in Italy. Much time was taken up by these bodies admonishing those parties who flouted these rules. The power and influence of the couture shows and

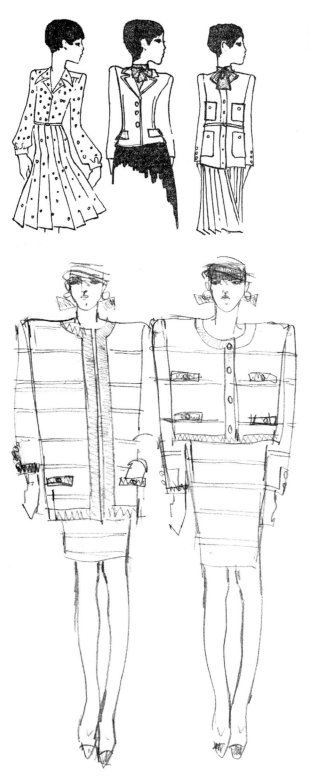

More images from Sylvia Ayton's sketchbook. Two generations of Wallis interpretations of Chanel – 1970s and 1980s.

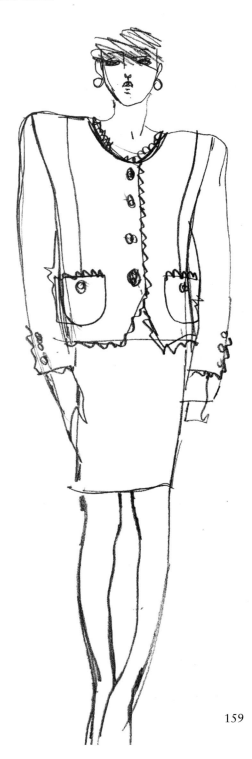

159

their impact on worldwide fashion cannot be overemphasised. The fortunes of wholesale fashion companies and garment manufacturers rose or fell by their ability to be the first to get a trend from the latest Paris couture show on to the high street. However, in the 1960s and 1970s the wholesale designer started creating original designs, not copied from great Paris couturiers, and the copying system began to fall apart.

Forecasting

Wholesale fashion companies and garment manufacturers had been happy with the old system because they knew how to work it. The new non-couture designers, later called the créateurs, made life difficult for garment manufacturers who could no longer copy the couture designs because they now looked dated and there was no system in place to copy their fellow, but rival, wholesale houses who now had the much more avant-garde and creative designers. Companies such as IM International in New York, Promostyle in Paris and Nigel French in London were able to cash in on this dilemma and create a service to inform wholesale fashion companies and garment manufacturers of the coming trends in silhouette, colour and fabric. These companies employed teams of young designers to scour the world for ideas, inspiration and research sources. By the 1970s the whole fashion package had become a great deal more sophisticated.

Photographers such as Richard Avedon, models such as Veruschka and magazines such as *Nova* and *Queen* created a fashion image that was much broader than just the single couture fashion item (which in the decade before could have made or broken a garment manufacturer). In 1954, Dior's H line dress was all that was needed to change world fashion; by 1970, a fashion image – the look, whether ethnic, peasant or androgynous – was the driving force that inspired the magazine reader and stimulated the market.

Each forecasting or prediction company has it own particular character or specialisation, but on the whole most companies use similar organisational patterns. Sections dealing with womenswear, menswear, sportswear and childrenswear have teams whose responsibility it is to oversee each of these sections. Textile design, printed, woven or knitted, together with the all-important aspects of colour, are also part of the company's remit, and special teams deal with these aspects. Meetings to coordinate ideas and conclusions are held regularly to give a consolidated picture of what is to come. In the past, forecasters were more daring and willing to risk new ideas in colour, texture, silhouette and fabrication, but with one or two burnt fingers in their history, companies are now more cautious and are, in fact, more likely to be trend indicators rather than predictors. Clients range from multinational garment manufacturers who have prediction schemes tailored to their particular needs, to smaller fashion companies who merely buy the expensive publications that most forecasting companies produce. Ideas are put forward at presentations either as PowerPoint slide shows or as glossy portfolios, or on internet sites, where all sections of their work are available, but clients can choose which section is most applicable to them – womenswear, knitwear, fashion prints, men's sportswear and so on.

With the emphasis now on trend indicators rather than the more risky forecasting, a shorter-term approach has become acceptable to clients. This means that couture houses have come back into their own as indicators. The fashion cycle from inspiration to the high street, although considerably shortened, is still a lengthy process and trends set by Galliano at Dior or Christian Lacroix are still viable currency for forecasters to use as trend indicators for at least two seasons ahead.

The copying and lifting that is so prevalent in the garment manufacturing industry can be done legally with help of the forecasting companies or illegally where manufacturers send their designers virtually as fashion spies to discover what designers are producing or actually to buy retail samples to copy. This is an area much

Above: prediction colours as displayed at the Première Vision trade fair in Paris.

Left: a prediction presentation at Première Vision.

Above: textile stands at Première Vision, and right, further prediction stands at Première Vision.

loved by the press but with no prospect of resolution.

The best known forecasting companies today are: the American WGSN (Worth Global Style Network) with a hugely comprehensive coverage of all aspects of fashion and lifestyle operating mainly through its excellent website; the Paris-based Promostyle, established much earlier than WGSN and which relies more heavily on its informative trend publications popular with buyers; and The Bureau in London which also selects key trends from the designer catwalks but in addition directs its clients to the broader socio-economic factors and tailors packages for specific companies like Harvey Nichols.

The fashion stylist

The stylist in fashion is a fairly new phenomenon. Stylists for interiors and photographic shoots for magazines have existed for a long time but in fashion, until recently, were deemed unnecessary. This was because the designer or fashion editor made the style decisions.

For fashion presentations, such as catwalk shows, accessories including hats, shoes, belts and bags and the general look were considered part of the designer's repertoire. More and more pressure on designers to present an event rather than a straightforward presentation of next season's models has meant that designers have had to turn to a new breed of fashion interpreters to style their shows. These stylists help produce catwalk shows where a much greater emphasis is placed on presentation techniques including make-up, accessorising, models, music and ambience.

Whereas in the past the fashion editor and her team decided on the items, photographer, look and location for a fashion shoot, the advent of a new wave of fashion magazines such as *The Face*, *Dazed and Confused*, *i-D* and *Arena* has changed the image-making techniques employed by magazines: 'a do-it-yourself approach to fashion that didn't rely on designer clothing to make a style statement', says Andrew Groves of the University of Westminster and former assistant designer to Alexander McQueen. Part of this new image-making requires the skills of the fashion stylist. 'Main brands such as Levis and Gap started to pay large amounts of money to high profile stylists such as Melanie Ward, Katie Grand and Katy England to enhance their large corporate brands with edgy, cool style. ... Many successful 'designers' now are actually more like stylists than designers as they model 'looks' rather than create original designs', adds Groves.

Even celebrities now use a fashion stylist rather than the advice of the designer to present themselves for a picture in a magazine or to receive an award. The choice of garment, make-up and accessories is left exclusively to the all-important and influential stylist.

The fashion educators – fashion schools

The influence of fashion education and fashion schools on the evolution of fashion in the second half of the twentieth century has been much greater than many operators in the field would admit – from the Chambre Syndicale School in Paris, to the impact of St Martin's School of Art in London on the current fashion scene, to the comparatively new but highly influential Flanders Fashion Institute in Antwerp.

Britain

The influence, excellence and fame of British fashion schools seem disproportionate to Britain's worldwide fashion reputation. The major institutions in this field have waxed and waned depending largely on the personality of the heads of departments. The Royal College of Art, St Martin's School of Art and Kingston were lucky to have dynamic personalities at the helm – the legendary Janey Ironside at the Royal College, the indomitable Muriel Pemberton at St Martin's and the outstanding and tireless Daphne Brooker at Kingston.

In many ways, without the Royal College

fashion school it is difficult to imagine that the 1960s fashion revolution would have had the influence and long-term effects that it did; Ossie Clark, Tuffin and Foale, and Anthony Price, who all trained at the RCA, had an enormous impact on the world scene. St Martin's, with its reputation for eccentricity, certainly produced some major influences; Rifat Osbek, John Galliano, Alexander McQueen and Stella McCartney have turned the world of fashion on its head. Kingston, with a slightly more work-a-day approach but always professional, produced not only many designers for the British fashion industry but also so many of the assistant designers to the top Italian design companies.

Harrow, Ravensbourne, Walthamstow, Middlesex, Newcastle and Gloucestershire were in the next league, but of the twenty-two colleges in Britain offering degree places in the 1970s and 1980s all were of an exceptional standard, a standard maintained by the now defunct CNAA, Council for National Academic Awards. It really is remarkable how British fashion education became the envy of the world. Standards in fashion design drawing, fashion illustration and innovative ideas are second to none.

France – the Chambre Syndicale Fashion School

The famous school of the Chambre Syndicale was the seed-bed from which so many great Paris designers developed and grew, such as André Courrèges, Dominique Sirop, Yves Saint Laurent, Issey Miyake and Valentino. Noted for its discipline and attention to the craft details, it offers a very formal and traditional curriculum to both French and foreign students. The two-year vocational course includes practical workshop placements and training in computer-aided design (CAD).

Belgium – Flanders Fashion Institute

In the late 1980s a set of young fashion designers that had studied at the Antwerp Academy of Fine Arts began to make their name on the fashion scene. The first intimation of this was when the 'Antwerp Six' showed in London in 1986. A joint venture between the Academy and the ITCB (Institute for Textiles and the Clothing Industry in Belgium) with Helena Ravijst as its driving force had produced designers such as Ann Demeulemeester, Dirk Bikkembergs, Martin Margiela and Dries Van Noten. The success of the school produced a second generation of talented designers, assuring the Antwerp Academy of its reputation. However, government reforms meant that the ITCB ceased to exist. The solution was to set up the FFI, Flanders Fashion Institute. In 1998 the FFI started to plan a building to house the fashion school, a museum, a library, an archive department, a forum and an institute all under one roof: the ModeNatie. The institute not only runs a fashion course but now houses international exhibitions in its impressive new building.

America – Parsons School of Design

Founded in 1896 by Frank Alvah Parsons expressly as a design school, its fashion department has an impressive list of ex-students. These include Adrian, Donna Karan, Claire McCardell, Isaac Mizrahi, Norman Norell and Anna Sui. This school, which is in Greenwich Village, New York, is at the cutting edge of design.

Italy – Camera Nazionale della Moda Italiana Fashion School

The Camera Nazionale della Moda Italiana, with the help of the region of Lombardy, set up a fashion school in Milan in 1997. The school aims to train young people in the specific skills required by the current fashion industry. The training is free and provided by the European Social Fund. Well-known design companies such as Mila Schon, Diesel and Versace have close links with the school.

Recruitment agencies

Designers at all levels need to find work, and a good designer will have probably worked for several different companies earning different and valuable experience from each. A designer who has this kind of experience is the most useful to a company as his/her knowledge and networking ability will be greater. To help designers find work, recruitment agencies like Denza International and In Design deal with companies all over the world who are looking for designers. Agencies like these will take designers on to their books and actively promote talent. The agencies visit student graduate shows to look for new talent – Graduate Fashion Week in London is a useful shop window for young student designers. On the whole, however, agents prefer designers with experience. There are many areas of work that agencies deal with: womenswear, menswear, children's wear, underwear and accessories are just some of these. Manufacturers will apply to these agencies to fill more technical and business posts as well as jobs in design.

Models and model agencies

The model is an indispensable part of fashion; without the model, clothes could not be fitted, tried out, appraised and shown to buyers. The public only sees the supermodels at spectacular events in the fashion capitals of the world, but there are models at all levels. Although there are both male and female models it is really the model girl who is most apparent as an adjunct to the fashion process.

The model girl

Despite talk of anorexia and exploitation of the young, the slim, perfectly proportioned figure of a model is of paramount importance. Not only does she have to be slim and tall but she must also have good shoulders, a small waist, slim hips and extra long legs: a glance at any fashion illustration over the past 60 years will tell you

The supermodel Erin models in Dries Van Noten's spring/summer 2003 show in Paris.

why – these attributes flatter the clothes. What is not realised is that if a garment is fitted on a model with these characteristics the garment will take on this shape and impart it to the less well-proportioned wearer.

Models can be showing or photographic; often a good showing model is not photogenic and a photographic girl may not be tall enough for showing.

Models at all levels are needed, and to this purpose there are model agencies in most cities. In the past, couture houses would employ house models, one or two on a permanent basis to do all the fittings and give small in-house showings. They would also hire several other model girls for the season. This, then, was the method for a girl to gain experience.

The top agents such as Models One in London or Elite in New York deal only with those girls who are likely to show on the international catwalks or be photographed for top fashion magazines or large advertising campaigns. Many models make their money from the much more mundane catalogue work, which nevertheless pays well. Other levels of model are used for trade fairs such as car shows, boat fairs and the many fashion fairs, for example The Clothes Show Live in Birmingham, UK.

The male model

In many ways the male model, from a fashion point of view, is less important than his female counterpart. It is quite possible for catwalk shows to take a man off the street, as long as he is tall enough, fairly good looking and can walk in a straight line. For photographic work, however, it is another story; the male model has to be extremely good-looking, photogenic, and have that extra something that can sell a product. In this area men can reach supermodel status, especially in huge advertising campaigns, as Werner Schreyer did with Hugo Boss in 1995.

The fashion calendar

The fashion calendar in principle relies on the sequence of events from concept to distribution: from yarn to the finished garment 'on the rail' in a store or other retail outlet. Each stage has to be researched, designed, sampled and shown to the potential customer who, of course, is different at each stage – the customer for the yarn producer is the textile manufacturer, the customer for the textile manufacturer is the garment designer and the customer for the garment designer is the retailer.

International fairs

International fairs enable the product to be shown to the appropriate customer at every stage; for example Pitti Filati in Florence for yarns usually takes place in February and July, Première Vision in Paris and Moda In in Milan for textiles usually take place in February and September and for garments the Prêt-à-Porter and designer shows in Paris, Moda Milano in Milan, London Fashion Week and New York Fashion Week take place in February/March for the autumn/winter of the same year and in September/October for the following spring/summer.

Another cycle altogether is the research, invention, design, manufacture and distribution of the new machinery required by the garment industry. This is a much longer process. Both heavy and light machinery is needed and every manufacturing process within the garment industry needs constant updating. Computer-aided systems, spreading tables, heavy pressing equipment, cutting tools, sewing machines and distribution systems are being redesigned and developed all the time. For this the IMB fair in Cologne, which is held every three years, is the biggest event of this kind in Europe and Bobbin in the USA is the equivalent for America.

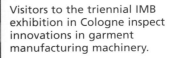

Visitors to the triennial IMB exhibition in Cologne inspect innovations in garment manufacturing machinery.

Timing

The calendar also depends on the intervals of time between each stage of the fashion/textile design process before the item can be manufactured in bulk. This process involves development, implementation, showing and distribution. It has to be remembered that the *samples* shown at yarn, textiles and fashion fairs are exactly that, samples – they have yet to go into mass production. Production is matched to orders as no manufacturer wants, or can afford, to produce items 'on spec'. The fairs are therefore where the orders are taken against samples. A substantial time lag occurs between placing the order for the yarn, textile or garment and receiving the goods. This is why the Prêt-à-Porter show and the ready-to-wear designer shows are held a year in advance, so that the designers can show their sample garments to the retailer, store or shop buyers who can in turn place their orders for selling in the shops, for the following year.

A two-year cycle

The two-year cycle preceded by yarn development and fabric research leads to the following sequence: fabric design, cloth sampling, cloth selection, cloth buying, fashion design, fashion sampling, buying/selection, ordering, manufacture and distribution.

As with many industries the manufacturing process in fashion is a long one. The various raw materials, which can be either natural such as cotton, linen, silk and wool, or man-made such as viscose, nylon, polyester and polypropylene, are the elements of the first stage of this process. Man-made fibres have to be scientifically developed before they can be converted into yarn. The yarn has to be designed and developed to introduce new properties such as stretch, texture, handle, durability and weight before it can be presented to the cloth manufacturer who will then weave it into cloth. The cloth samples, in turn, have to be presented to the fashion designers or garment manufacturers for them to make their cloth choices for the next season's collections. The designers then have to show their sample collections to buyers, working for stores or other retail outlets, who will select those items they want to present to the public in the following *season*. Each process takes approximately six months but the cycle from 'weaver to wearer' or, more precisely, from spinner to wearer is in excess of two years.

Sampling

International fairs are the main vehicle for yarn producers to show their products to the cloth manufacturers, for cloth manufacturers to show their samples to the designers and for designers to show their collections to the store buyers. This was not always the case. These specialist fairs have become more and more sophisticated over the past twenty years; before that there were other methods of showing samples to the appropriate companies. Cloth manufacturers would employ agents who would make appointments with the designers and garment manufacturers to show them their often vast collections. It has to be remembered that sample collections, especially in cloth, can be huge and are offered only in sample lengths. The actual fabric does not go into production until each cloth style has received sufficient orders to make its manufacture viable, and many fabric samples will never go into production. The selection stage of each of the industries, yarn, cloth and garment, is therefore vital to the healthy running of those industries. Without sufficient projected orders the yarn producers, cloth manufacturers and garment wholesalers would go out of business.

The couture cycle and other short cycles

The couture cycle is shorter than ready-to-wear and mass production because the professional store buyer's role is not part of the selling process – couture clothes are shown direct to the customer. Couture shows are held in January for spring/summer of that year and in July for autumn/winter of that same year.

Companies such as Zara, H&M and Next which have their own retail outlets can also shorten the cycle. Other experiments in shortening the cycle have been made using *just-in-time* technology or other electronically aided methods – a garment design can be faxed or e-mailed from London to Hong Kong, which can take days or even weeks off manufacturing time. Generally, however, the fashion industry is still geared up to the two-year cycle.

Coordination

The coordination of the different fairs is essential to the smooth running of a global fashion market, and a good fashion calendar is the tool that facilitates this exercise. This involves making sure that none of the fairs overlaps but that they are sufficiently close together to enable an overseas buyer to make one trip per season to see what is on offer in Paris, Milan, New York and London. The regulating bodies, such as the Chambre Syndicale, pioneered this and feel it is one of their primary functions. Many organisations and companies produce and publish fashion calendars which, depending on their specialisms or markets, will include more or less detail.

Fashion Monitor is a detailed source of news, contacts and events for the fashion, beauty and lifestyle industries. Published by the Profile Group (UK) Ltd, *Fashion Monitor* is relied on by PR consultancies, in-house press and PR officers, photographic, model and style agencies, retailers, the fashion and beauty media and event organisers.

The key dates on pages 170–72 have been extracted from *Fashion Monitor* and represent a snapshot of the extensive fashion industry calendar.

www.fashionmonitor.co.uk

KEY FASHION DATES 2003 – UK & INTERNATIONAL

JANUARY 12 2003
OVERSEAS

Milan Menswear Week (Milano Moda Uomo)
Various venues, Milan, Italy
Runs until: January 17 2003
International designer menswear collections for
autumn/winter 2003/4.
www.cameramoda.com
**Carla Ling, Camera Nazionale Della Moda Italiana 00 39 02 7600 0244
fax 00 39 02 784 033**

JANUARY 20 2003
OVERSEAS

Paris Haute Couture
Various venues, Paris, France
Runs until: January 23 2003
Paris' presentation of couture collections for spring/summer
2003 season. Catwalk shows and presentations are invitation-
only.
www.modeaparis.com
**Laurence Sudre-Monnier, Fédération Française de la Couture 00 33 1
4266 6444 fax 00 33 1 4266 9463**

JANUARY 24 2003
OVERSEAS

Prêt-à-Porter Paris
Paris Expo, Porte de Versailles, Paris, France
Runs until: January 27 2003
Key international fashion tradeshow previewing women's and
men's designer, classic and mainstream collections and
accessories for autumn/winter 2003/4. Around 1100
international exhibitors show within one of the 13 sections,
which include Atmosphère (designer collections), ...by Casabo
(designers newer to the market), and Première Classe (designer
accessories).
www.pretparis.com
**Michelle Jackson/Catherine Kimber, Promo Salons 020 8216 3100
fax 020 8447 1146**

Laurian Davies, UK Fashion Exports 020 7636 5577 fax 020 7636 7848

JANUARY 25 2003
OVERSEAS

Paris Menswear Week (Mode Masculine)
Various venues, Paris, France
Runs until: January 28 2003
International designer menswear catwalk collections for the
autumn/winter 2003/4 season.
www.modeaparis.com
**Laurence Sudre-Monnier, Fédération Française de la Couture 00 33 1
4266 6444 fax 00 33 1 4266 9463**

JANUARY 26 2003
OVERSEAS

Alta Roma – couture collections
L'Auditorium Parco della Musica, Rome, Italy
Runs until: January 30 2003
Rome's presentation of couture collections for spring/summer
2003 season. Catwalk shows and presentations are invitation-
only.
www.altamoda.it
Consuelo Aranyi, Alta Roma 00 39 06 678 1313 fax 00 39 06 6920 0303

FEBRUARY 5 2003
OVERSEAS

Pitti Immagine Filati
Fortezza da Basso, Florence, Italy
Runs until: February 7 2003
Biannual trade show previewing yarns for the knitted textiles
industry for the spring/summer 2004 season. Includes a trends
area, the Spazio Ricerca, and showcase of finished goods.
www.pittimmagine.com
David Harvey, Pitti Immagine 01491 612 381 fax 01491 612 381

FEBRUARY 7 2003
OVERSEAS

New York Fashion Week
Bryant Park, New York, USA
Runs until: February 14 2003
International fashion week featuring designer ready-to-wear
collections for the autumn/winter 2003/4 season. Includes
designer menswear collections – see separate entry.
www.7thonsixth.com
Jacquie Kelleher, 7th On Sixth 00 1 212 774 4307 fax 00 1 212 772 2617

New York Fashion Week – Menswear
Bryant Park, New York, USA
New York's catwalk event previewing international designer
menswear collections for the autumn/winter 2003/4 season.
Part of New York Fashion Week, which runs until February 14 –
see separate entry.
www.7thonsixth.com
Jacquie Kelleher, 7th on Sixth 00 1 212 774 4307 fax 00 1 212 772 2617

FEBRUARY 9 2003
OVERSEAS

MODA IN Tessuto & Accessori
Fiera Milano, Milan, Italy
Runs until: February 11 2003
Italy's main international trade fair dedicated to clothing textiles
and accessories, featuring spring/summer 2004 collections.
www.fieramodain.it
Mario de Luca, S.I. Tex 00 39 02 6610 3820 fax 00 39 02 6610 3844

FEBRUARY 11 2003

OVERSEAS

Indigo
Hall 6, Parc des Expositions, Paris Nord, Paris, France
Runs until: February 15 2003
International textile design tradeshow, incorporating knit, print and weave designs for seasons up to autumn/winter 2004/5. Part of Paris Pôle Mode.
www.indigo.tm.fr
Carol Jolley, Lille Chamber of Commerce 00 33 3 2063 7830 fax 00 33 3 2063 7834

Première Vision
Parc des Expositions, Paris Nord Villepinte, Paris, France
Runs until: February 15 2003
Major international tradeshow featuring fabrics and textile trends for spring/summer 2004. Part of Paris Pôle Mode.
www.premierevision.fr
Magali Ruard, PB Marketing Ltd 020 7221 3344 fax 020 7221 3446

Texworld Fabrics
CNIT La Défense, Paris, France
Runs until: February 14 2003
International textile show. Around 630 manufacturers from around the globe exhibit fabric collections and trends for spring/summer 2004. Incorporates Trends Forum.
www.texworld.messefrankfurt.com
Nathalie Pierron, Messe Frankfurt France 00 33 1 5526 8982 fax 00 33 1 4035 0900

FEBRUARY 15 2003

UK

London Fashion Week
Duke of York's Headquarters, King's Road, London, SW3
Runs until: February 20 2003
The UK's international fashion week featuring designer ready-to-wear collections for the autumn/winter 2003/4 season. Incorporates catwalk shows and the London Designers Exhibition, February 16–19.
www.londonfashionweek.co.uk
Sarah Thomas, Talk PR 020 7544 3853/4 fax 020 7543 4624

FEBRUARY 24 2003

OVERSEAS

Milan Fashion Week (Milano Moda Donna)
Various venues, Milan, Italy
Runs until: March 4 2003
Milan's international fashion week, previewing designer ready-to-wear womenswear collections for autumn/winter 2003/4.
www.cameramoda.it
Carla Ling, Camera Nazionale Della Moda Italiana 00 39 02 7600 0244 fax 00 39 02 784 033

MARCH 6 2003

OVERSEAS

Paris Fashion Week (Prêt-à-Porter)
Various venues, Paris, France
Runs until: March 14 2003
France's international fashion week, showcasing autumn/winter 2003/4 designer ready-to-wear womenswear collections.
www.modeaparis.com
Laurence Sudre-Monnier, Fédération Française de la Couture 00 33 1 4266 6444 fax 00 33 1 4266 9463

MAY 6 2003

OVERSEAS

IMB 2003
Exhibition Centre, Cologne, Germany
Runs until: May 10 2003
International tradeshow for apparel production, technology and textile processing industries.
www.imb.de
Tony Pittman, Kölnmesse GmbH UK Office 020 8681 8166 fax 020 8681 8028
Uwe Deitersen/Silvana Lai, Kölnmesse GmbH 00 49 221 821 2921/2307 fax 00 49 221 821 3423

JUNE 22 2003

OVERSEAS

Milan Menswear Week (Milano Moda Uomo)
Various venues, Milan, Italy
Runs until: June 27 2003
International designer menswear collections for spring/summer 2004.
www.cameramoda.com
Carla Ling, Camera Nazionale Della Moda Italiana 00 39 02 7600 0244 fax 00 39 02 784 033

JUNE 28 2003

OVERSEAS

Paris Menswear Week (Mode Masculine)
Various venues, Paris, France
Runs until: July 1 2003
International designer menswear catwalk collections for the spring/summer 2004 season.
www.modeaparis.com
Laurence Sudre-Monnier, Fédération Française de la Couture 00 33 1 4266 6444 fax 00 33 1 4266 9463

JULY 2 2003

OVERSEAS

Pitti Immagine Filati
Fortezza da Basso, Florence, Italy
Runs until: July 4 2003
Biannual trade show previewing yarns for the knitted textiles industry for the autumn/winter 2004/5 season. Includes a trends area and showcase of finished goods.
www.pittimmagine.com
David Harvey, Pitti Immagine 01491 612 381 fax 01491 612 381

JULY 7 2003

OVERSEAS

Paris Haute Couture
Various venues, Paris, France
Runs until: July 10 2003
Paris's presentation of couture collections for autumn/winter 2003/4 season. Catwalk shows and presentations are invitation-only.
www.modeaparis.com
Laurence Sudre-Monnier, Fédération Française de la Couture 00 33 1 4266 6444 fax 00 33 1 4266 9463

JULY 14 2003

OVERSEAS

Alta Roma – couture collections
L'Auditorium Parco della Musica, Rome, Italy
Runs until: July 18 2003
Rome's presentation of couture collections for autumn/winter 2003/4 season. Catwalk shows and presentations are invitation-only.
www.altamoda.it
Consuelo Aranyi, Alta Roma 00 39 06 678 1313 fax 00 39 06 6920 0303

SEPTEMBER 5 2003

OVERSEAS

Prêt à Porter Paris
Paris Expo, Porte de Versailles, Paris, France
Runs until: September 8 2003
Key international fashion tradeshow previewing women's and men's designer, classic and mainstream collections and accessories for spring/summer 2004. Around 1100 international exhibitors show within one of the 18 sections, which include Atmosphère (designer collections), ...by Casabo (designers newer to the market), and Première Classe (designer accessories).
www.pretparis.com
Michelle Jackson/Catherine Kimber, Promo Salons 020 8216 3100 fax 020 8447 1146
Laurian Davies, UK Fashion Exports 020 7636 5577 fax 020 7636 7848 info@ukfe.5portlandplace.org.uk

SEPTEMBER 9 2003

OVERSEAS

MODA IN Tessuto & Accessori
Fiera Milano, Milan, Italy
Runs until: September 11 2003
Italy's main international trade fair dedicated to clothing textiles and accessories, featuring autumn/winter 2004/5 collections.
www.fieramodain.it
Mario de Luca, S.I. Tex 00 39 02 6610 3820 fax 00 39 02 6610 3844

SEPTEMBER 12 2003

OVERSEAS

New York Fashion Week
Bryant Park, New York, USA
Runs until: September 19 2003International fashion week featuring designer ready-to-wear collections for the spring/summer 2004 season. Includes designer menswear collections – see separate entry.
www.7thonsixth.com
Jacquie Kelleher, 7th on Sixth/IMG 00 1 212 774 4307 fax 00 1 212 772 2617

New York Fashion Week – Menswear
Bryant Park, New York, USA
New York's catwalk event previewing international designer menswear collections for the spring/summer 2004 season. Part of New York Fashion Week, which runs until September 19 – see separate entry.
www.7thonsixth.com
Jacquie Kelleher, 7th on Sixth/IMG 00 1 212 774 4307 fax 00 1 212 772 2617

SEPTEMBER 16 2003

OVERSEAS

Texworld Fabrics
CNIT La Défense, Paris, France
Runs until: September 19 2003
International textile show. Over 600 manufacturers from around the globe exhibit fabric collections and trends for autumn/winter 2004/5. Incorporates Trends Forum.
www.texworld.messefrankfurt.com
Nathalie Pierron, Messe Frankfurt France 00 33 1 5526 8982 fax 00 33 1 4035 0900

SEPTEMBER 17 2003

OVERSEAS

Indigo
Hall 6, Parc des Expositions, Paris Nord, Paris, France
Runs until: September 20 2003
International textile design tradeshow, incorporating knit, print and weave designs for seasons up to spring/summer 2005. Part of Paris Pôle Mode.
www.indigo.tm.fr
Carol Jolley, Lille Chamber of Commerce 00 33 3 2063 7830 fax 00 33 3 2063 7834

Première Vision
Parc des Expositions, Paris Nord, Paris, France
Runs until: September 20 2003
Major international tradeshow featuring fabrics and textile trends for autumn/winter 2004/5. Part of Paris Pôle Mode.
www.premierevision.fr
Sonia Erhard, Première Vision UK 020 7537 3549 fax 020 7537 3549

SEPTEMBER 20 2003

UK

London Fashion Week
Duke of York's Headquarters, King's Road, London, SW3
Runs until: September 25 2003
The UK's international fashion week featuring designer ready-to-wear collections for the spring/summer 2004 season. Incorporates catwalk shows and the London Designers Exhibition, September 21–24.
www.londonfashionweek.co.uk
Sarah Thomas, Talk PR 020 7544 3853/4 fax 020 7544 3720

SEPTEMBER 27 2003

OVERSEAS

Milan Fashion Week (Milano Moda Donna)
Various venues, Milan, Italy
Runs until: October 5 2003
Milan's international fashion week, previewing designer ready-to-wear womenswear collections for spring/summer 2004.
www.cameramoda.com
Carla Ling, Camera Nazionale Della Moda Italiana 00 39 02 7600 0244 fax 00 39 02 784 033

OCTOBER 7 2003

OVERSEAS

Paris Fashion Week (Prêt-â-Porter)
Various venues, Paris, France
Runs until: October 15 2003
France's international fashion week, showcasing spring/summer 2004 designer ready-to-wear womenswear collections.
www.modeaparis.com
Laurence Sudre-Monnier, Fédération Française de la Couture 00 33 1 4266 6444 fax 00 33 1 4266 9463

Chapter 11
Considerations for the Future

Government initiatives – Financial backing – The need for a fully integrated
computer-aided system – Plagiarism – Can couture survive?

Government initiatives

Because for industrial nations the garment industry is a major producer of wealth and employment, governments have, to a greater or lesser degree, involved themselves in its well-being. Fashion's regulating bodies, such as the British Fashion Council, the Chambre Syndicale and Camera Nazionale della Moda Italiana, are part of larger organisations that involve government in their deliberations.

In Britain, for example, the Department of Trade and Industry, together with the British Apparel and Textile Association and its offshoot the British Fashion Council, have established the Textiles and Clothing Strategy Group (TCSG) as a forum to discuss the issues and challenges facing the sector. One of the tasks that the TCSB set itself was to study European fashion and production, and to decide whether government should be involved. Its first recommendation was that the 'DTI should press the European Commission to undertake a detailed study into the reasons for the relative success of the Italian clothing industry and the relative decline of the clothing industries in Germany, France and the UK'.

There are many ways in which government can help indirectly, through taxation methods and funding research in industry and universities, and directly by funding government training schemes.

Financial backing

So far, Britain has done particularly badly in attracting private funding, failing its young designers who have been unable to sustain their initial successful impact, through lack of sound financial backing. In France and Italy it is quite a different story: British designers such as McQueen, McCartney and Galliano have been taken up and nurtured by the huge international conglomerates. In France, a model has been established where business design partners (for example Bergé at Yves Saint Laurent) have lent such confidence to both finance companies and shareholders that it is no wonder Christian Lacroix was encouraged by Financière Agache to set up his couture house. Philip Green's initiative at Top Shop could be Britain's guide to the future.

The need for a fully integrated computer-aided system

The modern fashion industry is now a global operation. A garment designed in London can be manufactured in Taiwan from fabric woven in Italy and then distributed to the USA in a very short time. Due to different and often unexpected aspects of modern technology – the availability of e-mail and the fax machine, for example – design modification can now be virtually instantaneous and worldwide. A sample made and bought in Paris can be copied in Turkey, approved in London, manufactured in the Far East and distributed throughout Europe with equal facility and still labelled as a UK product. Manufacturers in Taiwan, Hong Kong and Turkey are now rarely the fashion sweatshops of the past but sophisticated, computer-aided manufacturing units.

Despite this, computer-aided design and manufacture (CAD/CAM) systems are still not fully vertically integrated into the fashion design, pattern cutting and manufacturing sequence. The design stage, not understood or catered for by CAD/CAM systems producers, has been left out. This omission is the result of misunderstanding the design process – ignoring its most salient qualities, giving it qualities it does not have and forgetting to include fashion designers in the planning and design of these systems. It is interesting to note that the only system to date to touch on the requirements of designers was created by a fashion designer to meet her own needs. Fashion does not yet have a CAD system linked to a CAM system comparable to the facilities available in similar product design disciplines.

Research is under way to overcome some of these difficulties. Software companies are developing systems to incorporate design and technology. Fashion schools are introducing specialist pathways, for example fashion design with product development, from which a new breed of fashion technologists should emerge.

Plagiarism

Copying may be so much a part of the fashion process that, no matter how much regulation is supposed to govern copyright, it may be impossible ever to counteract plagiarism in fashion. The promotion of the success of shorter lead times from catwalk to high street has meant that the original designers' input and their protection seems to have been quite forgotten. One positive step is that companies such as Top Shop and Debenhams are employing the designers themselves to create new ranges.

Can couture survive?

Because of its new lease of life as the vehicle of the avant-garde, couture today is probably in a better position than it has been for years. That the giant conglomerates like LVMH think it worth supporting houses such as Dior and Givenchy with designers that cannot by any stretch of the imagination be thought of as commercial is surely a sign of this.

Appendix I
The Incorporated Society of London Fashion Designers (Britain)

The following is an extract from an article by the author on the Incorporated Society that was published in *Costume*, the journal of the Costume Society, No. 35, in 2001.

The Incorporated Society of London Fashion Designers was launched during the Second World War to encourage and revive Britain's clothing export market and set standards of workmanship and design protection for London couturiers. Although primarily established to foster and develop the couture market, it had a huge influence on fashion design, manufacture and distribution at all levels and for over twenty years was the only arbiter of design in British fashion. However, since the explosion of interest in fashion of the sixties, the significance of the Incorporated Society has largely been forgotten. The Society was founded with the prompting of Alison Settle of *Vogue* in 1942 by Sir Cecil Weir of the Board of Trade for 'government to deal with one group instead of separate ones on fashion promotion.' The leading designers of that year, Hardy Amies, Norman Hartnell, Digby Morton, Bianca Mosca, Peter Russell, Victor Stiebel and Elspeth Champcommunal at Worth of London gathered under the leadership of Mrs Ashley Havinden of W.S. Crawford Ltd, the advertising agency, with the help of Mr Yoxall of *Vogue*. They discussed the idea outlined by Sir Cecil Weir and decided to form themselves into a group that was to be known as The Incorporated Society of London Fashion Designers. They set themselves three main aims: a) To maintain and develop the reputation of London as a centre of fashion. b) To collaborate with groups of fabric and other manufacturing firms and individuals with a view to increasing the prestige of Britain and promoting the sales of British fashions in the home and overseas markets. c) To assist fashion designers by protecting their original designs and enabling them to exchange information to their mutual advantage, arranging co-ordinated showing dates, fostering professional and trade interests, developing standards of skilled workmanship and representing their views to government, trade bodies and the Press.

Although commonly known as the 'top ten' the number of designers varied over the years. Also from the article is the entire membership of designers with biographical notes. Sadly, since the article was published in 2001, Hardy Amies and John Cavanagh have died.

Sir Hardy Amies KCVO

Born in 1909, he was a founder member of the Incorporated Society of London Fashion Designers, which he joined and helped launch in 1942. He had previously worked as the designer for Lachasse. He started up his own house at 14 Savile Row in November 1945. Dressmaker by Appointment to the Queen. Vice-Chairman of the Society 1954–56 and Chairman 1959–60.

John Cavanagh

Born in Ireland in 1914 but educated at St Paul's School, London. Trained at and later assistant to Edward Molyneux he also worked as assistant to Pierre Balmain in Paris; started up on his own at 26 Curzon Street in 1952 and became member of the Society in the same year. Vice-Chairman 1956–59.

Clive

Clive Evans trained at Canterbury School of Art, worked at Lachasse and finally, after winning a prestigious competition, set up on his own at 17 Saint George's Street in 1970.

Charles Creed

The son of Henry Creed and the grandson of another Henry who had introduced women's tailoring to Paris from their house in Place de l'Opéra in the 1890s. Charles continued the tradition at 31 Basil Street in London until his death in 1966. He was a founder member and joined in 1942. He married Pat Cunningham who later became an editor of *Vogue*.

Angèle Delanghe

Joined the Incorporated Society in 1945 but had to give up her establishment in April 1947 due to financial difficulties. She rejoined the Society in April 1961. Noted for her soft, feminine tailored clothes, beautiful romantic eveningwear and wedding dresses. Her house was at 22 Bruton Place.

Sir Norman Hartnell

Founder member joined in 1942 but had run a most successful house at 26 Bruton Street since the early 1920s. Couturier to the Queen and the Queen Mother. His dresses for the Coronation were world famous. Several times President of the Society. Born 1901, died 1979.

Lachasse

Founded in 1929 by a Mrs Phillips at 4 Farm Street and, as its name suggests, was the sports boutique of the couture house Gray and Paulette in Berkeley Square, owned and run by Frederick Shingleton who had earlier bought the Paris house of Paulette. A training ground for many of the Society's designers: Digby Morton, Hardy Amies, Michael, Owen and Clive. The house still continues today in South Kensington under the leadership of Peter Lewis Crown. The house became a member of the Society in 1950.

Mattli

Guiseppe Gustave known to the fashion world as 'Jo', the house was simply called Mattli. Born in Switzerland and trained in Paris with Premet he opened his own house in London in 1934. There is no record of when Mattli joined the Society but it must have been early on in its life as he is recorded as being present at Society meetings in the early 1940s. In later years he shared premises with Charles Creed at 31 Basil Street. Born in 1907, he died 1982.

Michael

Born in Ireland, Michael Donellan, simply known as Michael, designed at Lachasse where he followed Digby Morton and Hardy Amies as designer. Founded his own house in 1953 when he took over Peter Russell's business at 2 Carlos Place. He joined the Society in 1954. Called by *Vogue* 'the Balenciaga of London'.

Edward Molyneux

Known as the Captain from his First World War rank, Irish by birth, he opened his house in Paris at 14 Rue Royal in 1919. His impeccable clothes were known for their understated chic. During the war he moved to London but afterwards returned to Paris where his house survived until the mid sixties. Later in the decade Yves Saint Laurent did a complete collection based on his look. He was a founder member of the Society and resigned in 1947 when his sister Kathleen took over the running of the house. Died in Monte Carlo in 1974.

Digby Morton

A founder member of the Society; came from Dublin where he had studied architecture. Joined Lachasse in 1933. Famous for his tailored suits, in 1934 he opened his own couture house. Born in 1906 he retired in 1973. His glamorous wife, Phyllis, helped run his business and often compèred fashion shows, including those of the Society. Died in 1983.

Bianca Mosca

A founder member, of Italian origin she had worked for Schiaparelli in Paris before moving to London in 1939 to direct the Jacqmar studio. She opened her own couture house in 1946. In private life she was Mrs Claude Crawford; her flair for interior design was recorded in an article about her in *Vogue* in June 1949.

Ronald Paterson

A Scot, born in 1917, from Bridge of Allan in Stirlingshire he studied fashion at the Piccadilly Institute of Design. He joined the Society in 1953 and was Vice-Chairman for some years. His elegant house was at 25 Albemarle St.

Peter Russell

A founder member who had been established in London before the Second World War. His house at 2 Carlos Place was taken over by Michael when Peter Russell decided to start up a new business in Australia in 1953.

Michael Sherard

Started his London couture house in 1946, became a member of the Society in 1949. His house at 17 Curzon Street closed in 1964. He later became the Director of the London College of Fashion.

Victor Stiebel

Born in South Africa in 1907. Came to England in 1924 where he studied architecture at Jesus College, Cambridge. Trained with Reville in London and started his own house in Bruton Street in 1932; he later moved to magnificent premises at 17 Cavendish Square. A founder member of the Society of which for a period he was Vice-President. He closed his house in June 1959 and died in 1976.

Worth of London

An offshoot of the famous Paris couture house founded by Charles Frederick Worth in 1858. The London branch was opened in the time of Queen Victoria. Elspeth Champcommunal, Mrs Mortimer and Owen Hyde Clarke were the designers during the time of the Incorporated Society and as such the house was a founder member.

The Chambre Syndicale de la Couture Parisienne (France)

The following description is based on the official website, www.modeaparis.com, of the Fédération Française de la Couture du Prêt-à-Porter des Couturiers et des Créateurs de Mode.

Organisation

The Chambre Syndicale de la Couture Parisienne is now part of a larger organisation, the Fédération Française de la Couture du Prêt-à-Porter des Couturiers et des Créateurs de Mode. The Chambre Syndicale, as it is usually known, set the pattern for similar organisations, e.g. the British Incorporated Society of London Fashion Designers and the Italian Camera Nazionale dell'Alta Moda Italiana, both much younger, but only the Chambre and Camera have survived.

The Fédération was constituted in 1973 and is made up of three Chambres Syndicales: the Chambre Syndicale de la Couture Parisienne created in 1868 for the couturiers, the Chambre Syndicale du Prêt-à-Porter des Couturiers et des Créateurs set up in 1973 for the ready-to-wear designers, and the Chambre Syndicale de la Mode Masculine for the menswear designers also set up in 1973. The Union Nationale Artisanale de la Couture et des Activités Connexes, representing the craftsmen and women of the profession, became a 'corresponding member' of the Fédération in 1975.

Aims

(1) To establish a calendar or timetable working in concert with the press, which makes sure that the show dates and times are coordinated to allow the press and buyers to cover all the collections in a season. The calendar is sent out to journalists, French and foreign buyers and to commercial establishments.

(2) To make a comprehensive registered *press list* of those organisations whose directors have agreed to the rules and regulations set down for journalists accredited by the Chambre Syndicale so that official invitations to the shows can be sent to them.

(3) A long-standing objective of the Fédération has been to show all the prêt-à-porter collections under one roof to make the job of journalists from both home and abroad easier. In 1976 this was achieved for the first time where the majority of designers of the Fédération presented their prêt-à-porter collections at the Palais des Congrès. In subsequent years the shows have been held in various venues in Paris and more recently in le Carrousel du Louvre. The prêt-à-porter collections are shown in March and October and over 2000 journalists and 800 buyers attend each season.

Organised events abroad

The member houses of the Fédération earn about 70% of their turnover in exports. The Fédération's major purpose is to help maintain and develop the fashion industry on the international markets. To this end, every year the Fédération organises events such as group fashion shows, showcasing the different styles of various fashion and couture designers. These group events promote not only the ready-to-wear and haute couture garments displayed in the shows, but also the overall commercial products of French fashion designers and couturiers.

French cultural and promotional events

Those who organise cultural and promotional events are often interested in gaining sponsorships from well-known French fashion labels. Indeed, for the public and especially the international public, these names symbolise the high quality and inventiveness of French products and attest to a successful partnership between art and industry.

Press promotion

The Fédération acts as mediator between the press and the fashion industry. It also helps organise and advertise events that promote the ever-changing nature of France's fashion industry such as providing stands at fashion shows for the press and organising collective advertising in international magazines.

Public relations

Relations with public services and the government

Like any other professional body, the Fédération acts as spokesperson for the fashion industry to public services and the government.

Relations with management and labour forces

The Chambre Syndicale de la Couture, which signed the Convention Collective de la Couture Parisienne (Parisian Couture Collective Agree-ment), regularly negotiates with trade unions on salary and employment matters.

Information and advice to members

The Fédération also informs and advises its members on legislation and regulations concerning economy, tax and trade.

Defence of artistic copyright

Fashion designers are frequently victims of forgery (illegal copies of their creations, counterfeited labels or illicit use of labels). These practices are detrimental to the entire fashion industry. The Fédération works in close collaboration with the government and all related public services to fight any kind of forgery in France, in the EC or elsewhere. The research led by the Comité National Anti-Contrefaçon (Anti-Counterfeiting National Committee), part of the Ministry of Economy, Finance and Industry, deals especially with forgery matters. Current examples are examined in order to improve legislation abroad and make it similar to French legislation, which is particularly efficient.

Vocational training

The schools attached to the Chambre Syndicale de la Couture provide training courses and also enable young people to become acquainted with the techniques of the industry as well as the French fashion world. The Fédération is a member of the FORTHAC, a registered fund-raising body operating on a shared management basis. The FORTHAC is composed of the textile, garment and fine leather craft industries. Its mission is to collect the firms' in-house training tax and to develop an incentive policy on training matters. Together with its partners in the textile and garment industry, the Fédération has founded an association called FITHAC, which manages the administration of in-house training of fashion houses situated in the Île-de-France.

Appendix III
The Camera Nazionale della Moda Italiana (Italy)

The Camera Nazionale dell'Alta Moda Italiana works under the umbrella of the larger Camera Nazionale della Moda Italiana but deals exclusively with alta moda or haute couture. The following is based on the Camera Nazionale della Moda Italiana's own description of its organisation taken from its promotional literature and website (www.cameramoda.it).

Camera Nazionale della Moda Italiana is the non-profit-making association that governs, coordinates and promotes the development of Italian fashion.

It represents the highest cultural values of Italian fashion, and its aim is to protect, coordinate and enhance its image, both in Italy and abroad.

In accordance with the provisions of its bye-laws, the association is the reference, the privileged point of contact for all the domestic and international activities aimed at enhancing the value of and promoting Italian style, customs and fashion.

Ever since it was founded, in 1958, it has implemented in time a policy of organised support, furthering knowledge, promoting and developing fashion, by means of prestigious events for its image, in Italy and abroad.

The recent agreements concerning international schedules which have led to the signature of a joint French and Italian protocol have given Milan and Camera Nazionale della Moda Italiana the role of undisputed leading player on the international fashion stage, thus contributing also towards the consolidation of the alliances already forged with London and New York.

The Franco-Italian protocol signed in Paris on 26th June 2000 is founded on the precise intention of the Camera Nazionale della Moda Italiana and the Fédération Française de la Couture to implement a common policy aimed at developing and circulating luxury products in non-European areas.

In particular the protocol tends to form a common Italian and French front on the following issues (as well as on the schedules of events):

- fighting counterfeiting;
- co-operation in the field of professional training;
- promotion of Italian and French products in non-European markets.

In the fashion macroeconomic system, the Camera Nazionale della Moda Italiana represents 200 firms that are the top of the sector as a whole.

The firms that belong to the association have the common goal of promoting Italian brands and Italian products. Since it does not represent the category as a whole, the association leaves it up to other organisations to concern themselves with trade-union and legal issues.

The Camera Nazionale della Moda Italiana includes firms active in the following fields: haute couture, prêt-à-porter, fabrics, textile/clothing industries, accessories, leatherwear, footwear, furs, sportswear, hard accessories, distribution, cosmetics, circuses and theatrical costumes.

Fashion shows

- Milano Moda Uomo autumn/winter (January)
- Milano Moda Donna autumn/winter (February–March)
- Milano Moda Uomo spring/summer (June–July)
- Milano Moda Donna spring/summer (September–October)
- AltaRoma (January–July) The Italian couturiers' show in Rome – the AltaRoma – includes many new designers but some names are familiar from the past like Lancetti, Egon Von Furstenberg and Renato Balestra.

Appendix IV
America

The Fashion Group International (America)

This organisation, which in many ways is the American equivalent of the Chambre Syndicale and the Camera Nazionale della Moda Italiana, has a similar but different role in supporting American fashion. In 1928 at the instigation of Edna Woolman Chase, editor-in-chief of *American Vogue*, seventeen influential fashion business-women met in a small New York restaurant to conceive a plan to set up an American Fashion Organisation. Its aim was primarily 'to provide a forum to express and enhance a widening awareness of the American fashion business and women's role in that business'. By 1930, the organisation became a reality. Given an office from which to operate by Louis Fairchild in his *Women's Wear Daily* office on East 12 Street in New York, Fashion Group International (FGI) set out its working agenda: to have a dedicated purpose, a set of regulations and bye-laws, appointed officials and a membership policy.

The founding members were impressive: Elizabeth Arden, Margaret Case, Eleanor Roosevelt, Helena Rubenstein, Julia Coburn, Lilly Daché, Jessica Daves, Nan Danskin, Edith Head, Eleanor LeMaire, Claire McCardell, Clare Potter, Virgina Pope, Dorothy Shaver, Adele Simpson, Carmel Snow and Miss Tobé.

FGI's second home was at 572 Madison Avenue provided by *Harpers Bazaar*, but by 1934 it had moved to 300 Rockerfeller Centre. Today FGI is to be found at 597 Fifth Avenue.

The Group's aims were and still are straight-forward: the advancement of professionalism in fashion, the provision of a public forum for contemporary fashion issues, the presentation of fashion trends, the recognition of business-women's achievements, the promotion of career opportunities, the provision of an inter-fashion networking system, and to administer the FGI Foundation. This Foundation was set up to promote fashion education, provide scholarships and career counselling and sponsor educational seminars.

Council of Fashion Designers of America

Another American body with a similar function is the Council of Fashion Designers of America (CFDA). It was founded in 1962 as a non-profit-making trade association 'to further the position of fashion design as a recognised branch of American art and culture, to advance its artistic and professional standards, to establish and maintain a code of ethics and practices of mutual benefit in professional, public, and trade relations, and to promote and improve public understanding and appreciation of the fashion arts through leadership in quality and taste'. Membership is by invitation.

The founding members of CFDA were Bill Blass, Donald Brooks, Betty Carol, Jane Derby, Luis Estevez, David Evins, Rudi Gernreich, Bud Kilpatrick, Helen Lee, Jean Louis, John Moore, Norman Norell, Sylvia Pedlar, Sarmi, Arnold Scaasi, Adele Simpson, Gustave Tassell, Pauline Trigère, Sydney Wragge and Ben Zuckerman.

Bibliography

Aldrich, Winifred (1992) *CAD in Clothing and Textiles*. Blackwell Scientific Publications, Oxford.

Aldrich, Winifred (2000) Tailor's cutting manuals and the growing provision of popular clothing 1770–1870. *Textile History*, No. 31.

Amies, Hardy (1954) *Just So Far*. Collins, London.

Anstey, Helen and Weston, Terry (1997) *Guide to Textile Terms*. Weston Publishing, London.

Apparel International. Piel-Caru Publishing, England.

Arch, Nigel and Marschner, Joanna (1987) *Splendour at Court*. Unwin Hyman, London.

Battersby, Martin (1974) *Art Deco Fashion*. Academy Editions, London.

Beaton, Cecil (1954) *The Glass of Fashion*. Cassell, London.

Beaton, Cecil (1971) *Fashion*. V&A Publications, London.

Belle Assemblée, Vol. X, London. 1839.

Benaim, Laurence (2002) *Debut Yves Saint Laurent*. Abrams, New York.

Birtwell, Celia (1999) *Ossie Clark*. Warrington Museum and Art Gallery.

Blum, Daniel (1968) *A Pictorial History of the Talkies*. Spring Books, London.

Brighton Museum and Bath City Council (1985) *Norman Hartnell*. Brighton Museum and Bath City Council.

Chenoune, Farid (1993) *A History of Men's Fashion*. Flammarion, Paris.

Coleman, Elizabeth Ann (1983) *The Genius of Charles James*. Brooklyn Museum, New York.

Coleman, Elizabeth Ann (1990) *The Opulent Era: Fashions of Worth, Doucet and Pingat*. Thames & Hudson, New York.

Coleridge, Nicholas (1998) *The Fashion Conspiracy*. Heinemann, London.

Creed, Charles (1961) *Maid to Measure*. Jarrolds, London.

de Courcy, Anne (2000) *The Viceroy's Daughters*. Weidenfeld & Nicholson, London.

De la Haye, Amy and Glenville, Tony (1996) *The Cutting Edge: 50 Years of British Fashion 1947–1997*. V&A Publications, London.

De la Haye, Amy and Wilson, Elizabeth (1999) *Defining Dress*. Manchester University Press.

Drapers Record. Emap Fashion Ltd, London.

Dupire, Beatrice and Sy, Hady (1998) *Yves Saint Laurent: Forty Years of Creation*. International Festival of Fashion Photography, USA.

Duras, Marguerite (1988) *Yves Saint Laurent*. Ebury Press, London.

Ehrlich, Blake (1968) *London*. Cassell, London.

Emporio Armani Magazine. Armani Press, Milan.

Ewing, Elizabeth (1974) *A History of Twentieth Century Fashion*. Batsford, London.

Fogg, Marnie (2003) *Boutique*. Mitchell Beazley, London.

Ginsburg, Madeleine (1980) *Fashion Illustration*. V&A Publications, London.

Ginsburg, Madeleine (1990) *The Hat*. Studio Editions, London.

Gorman, Paul (2001) *The Look*. Sanctuary Publishing, London.

Harpers Bazaar. National Magazine Co. Ltd, London.

Hartnell, Norman (1955) *Silver and Gold*. Evans Brothers, London.

Howell, Georgina (1990) *Sultans of Style*. Ebury Press, London.

Howell, Georgina (1991) *In Vogue: 75 Years of Style*. Condé Nast, London.

HRH The Duke of Windsor (1960) *Windsor Revisited*. Riverside Press, Cambridge.

Ironside, Janey (1968) *A Fashion Alphabet*. Michael Joseph, London.

Jenkyn Jones, Sue (2002) *Fashion Design*. Laurence King, London.

Jouve, Marie-Andrée (1997) *Balenciaga*. Thames & Hudson, London.

Kahane, Eric (1961) *Un Marriage Parisien Sous le Directoire*. Editions Le Carrousel, Paris.

Lancaster, Osbert (1951) *London Night and Day*. The Architectural Press, London.

Langley Moore, Doris (1949) *Gallery of Fashion 1790–1822*. Batsford, London.

Latour, Anny (1958) *Kings of Fashion*. Weidenfeld & Nicolson, London.

Martin, Paul (1967) *European Military Uniforms*. Spring Books, London.

McDowell, Colin (1984) *McDowell's Directory of Twentieth Century Fashion*. Frederick Muller, London.

McDowell, Colin (1997) *Forties Fashion*. Bloomsbury, London.

McDowell, Colin (1997) *Galliano*. Weidenfeld & Nicolson, London.

Mendes, Valerie (1984) *John French*. V&A Publications, London.

Mendes, Valerie (1990) *Pierre Cardin Past Present and Future*. Dirk Nishen, London.

Morris, Bernadine (1978) *The Fashion Makers*. Random House, New York.

Mulvagh, Jane (1988) *Vogue History of 20th Century Fashion*. Viking, London.

Mulvagh, Jane (1998) *Vivienne Westwood*. Harper Collins, London.

Musée des Arts de la Mode (1986) *Hommage à Christian Dior*. Union des Arts Décoratifs, Paris.

Musée des Arts de la Mode (1986) *Yves Saint Laurent*. Editions Herscher, Paris.

Nicolas, Madeleine (1977) *Elégance et Création*. Palais Galliéra, Paris.

Nicolas, Madeleine (1981) *La Mode et ses Métiers*. Palais Galliéra, Paris.

Nuzzi, Cristina (1980) *Fashion in Paris*. Thames and Hudson, London.

Packer, William (1989) *Eric*. Webb and Bower, Exeter.

Paulvé, Dominique and Boyé, Marie (2001) *In Fashion*. Cassell, London.

Pochna, Marie-France (1996) *Dior*. Thames and Hudson, London.

Polan, Brenda (1983) *The Fashion Year*. Zomba Books, London.

Praz, Mario (1982) *An Illustrated History of Interior Decoration*. Thames & Hudson, London.

Queen. Stevens Press, London.

Rhodes, Zandra and Knight, Anne (1984) *The Art of Zandra Rhodes*. Zandra Rhodes Publications, London.

Ritchie, Berry (1990) *A Touch of Class*. James & James, London.

Sanderson, Elizabeth (2001) The new dresses: a look at how mantua making became established in Scotland. *Costume, The Journal of the Costume Society* 35.

Service, Alastair (1979) *London 1900*. Granada, London.

Tapert, Annette and Edkins, Diana (1995) *The Power of Style*. Aurum Press, London.

Textile View. David R. Shah, Amsterdam.

The Fashion Book. Phaidon, London. 1998.

The New Yorker, Condé Nast, New York.

Vionnet. Judith Clark Costume, London. 2001.

Vreeland, Diana (1984) *D.V.* (Plimpton, George and Hemphil, Christopher, eds). Weidenfeld & Nicholson, London.

Vogue. Condé Nast, New York and Paris.

Waddell, G. (2001) The Incorporated Society of Fashion Designers. *Costume, The Journal of the Costume Society*, No. 35.

Walker, Richard (1989) *Savile Row*. Rizzoli, New York.

Wallach, Janet (1999) *Chanel*. Mitchell Beazley, London.

Useful Addresses and Websites

Trade periodicals in the UK

Draper's Record
Retail Week
Menswear
Menswear Buyer
Bridal Buyer
Textile View

(These publications can be obtained from R.D. Franks, Kent House, Market Place, Oxford Circus, London W1 8EJ. Tel: 020 7636 1244)

Recruitment agencies

Denza International, www.denza.co.uk

Indesign, 1 Ashland Place, London W1. Tel: 020 7935 7485. www.indesignrecruitment.co.uk

Star Executives, 7 Fitzroy Mews, London W1 6DQ. Tel: 020 7387 6969

Useful websites

American fashion information – http://fashion.about.com/mbody.htm
Brioni, Italian tailor – http://www.brioni.it/english/eventirig.htm
British clothing directory – http://www.britishcompanies.co.uk/ adultclothing.htm
Camera Nazionale della Moda Italiana – http://www.cameramoda.it/
Department of Trade and Industry, Clothing Footwear and Fashion Sector, UK –
    http://www.dti.gov.uk/sectors_clothing.html
Fashion Group International, USA – http://www.fgi.org
Fashion Monitor – http://www.fashionmonitor.co.uk/
Fashion-411 Fashion Trends, Magazines and Shopping Guides – http://www.fashion-411.com/index.html
Federated Department Stores Inc. – Bloomingdale's, Macy's, Le Bon Marché –
    http://www.fds.com/retail/blo_2_3.asp
Fédération Française de la Couture, du Prêt-à-Porter des Couturiers et des Créateurs de Mode (Chambre
    Syndicale) – http://www.modeaparis.com/va/index.html
Flanders Fashion Institute (FFI) Antwerp – http://www.ffi.be/
IMB tri-annial technology fair, Cologne – http://www.imb-forum.de
Italian fashion archives – http://associazioni.comune.firenze.it/ archiviogiorgini/
Italian fashion design website – http:// www.made-in-italy.com/fashion/index.html
Italian fashion directory – http://search.modaitalia.net/
Italian textile directory – http://www.yellowtex.com/
Kilgour French Stanbury, Savile Row tailor – http://www.8savilerow.com/
Le Bon Marché, Rive Gauche, Paris – http://www.lebonmarche.fr/
Mary Quant – http://www.maryquant.co.jp/
Moda In, Italian textile fair – http://www.modain.it/htm/home.asp
Philip Treacy – http://www.philiptreacy.co.uk/flash/ welcome2.html

Pitti Immagine trade fairs – http:// www.pittimmagine.com/_ENG/index2.html

Première Vision, French textile fair – http://www.premierevision.fr/gb/index.html

Prêt-à-Porter, French ready-to-wear womenswear fair – http://www.pretparis.com/default.asp

Samaritaine store, Paris – http://www.lasamaritaine.com

Textile Clothing Technology Corporation – http://www.tc2.com/index.htm

View (Textile View) email: office@view-publications.com

Vogue and *W*, USA – http://www.style.com/

Vogue, UK – www.vogue.com

Worth Global Style Network (WGSN) is free to fashion students who are on a registered fashion course – http://www.wgsn-edu.com/edu/index.htm

Glossary

Alteration hand	A seamstress or sewing operative employed to make alterations to ready-to-wear garments, usually to make them fit.
Argyll	(1) A type of tartan usually used on socks. (2) A type of men's topcoat that has a cape.
Assembly	The making or putting together of a garment.
Atelier	(1) Workroom in a couturier's, from the French for studio. (2) Dressmaking hand, i.e. workroom staff.
Balance	(1) One of the apparently mystic words in both couture and dressmaking which means crudely that the front is the same length as the back or that the hem, waistline and bust line are parallel to the floor. (2) Without balance the garment will not hang properly.
Band knife	One of the mechanical aids that cut out several layers of cloth at once; a single revolving blade with a protective cover.
Basting	Another term for tacking, marking out or temporarily sewing together by hand with a needle and thread.
Battle dress	Soldiers' 'undress' uniform with waist-length, slightly bloused jacket with a waist band and box-pleated pockets.
Beast	The item in every collection which, no matter how many alterations and adjustments are made, just will not work.
Bespoke	Made to measure to the customer's individual measurements especially in men's tailoring.
BFC	The British Fashion Council, which organises London Fashion Week and the annual British Fashion Awards and comes under the overall control of the British Apparel and Textile Confederation (BATC).
Bias cut	A cutting technique to make woven fabric more fluid or elastic whereby it is cut 'on the cross' or at 45 degrees to the vertical selvedge. See Chapter 8, Madeleine Vionnet. See also **flou**.
Binding	A method of finishing a fabric edge often in **self-cloth**.
Blind hemmer	A machine used in mass production that can replicate the qualities of a hand-finished hem.
Blocks	(1) Perfected pattern templates of basic parts of a garment – bodice, sleeve, skirt and collar – from which a pattern can be drafted. There can also be trouser blocks, jacket blocks, coat blocks and dress blocks.

(2) Hat blocks: the wooden or metal shapes used in millinery to mould the hat shape, usually by steaming.

Block makers
The craftspeople who make hat blocks.

Bobbin
The world's largest garment production fair held in America.

Body
Another term for the dressmaker's or tailor's dummy – a padded and fabric covered shape that simulates the human body – on to which the pattern, toile or garment in its different stages of completion can be pinned, fitted and appraised.

Breeches
Short trousers fastened below the knee later used as the term for trousers. Many of the great tailors originally called themselves breeches makers.

Brim
That part of a hat that encircles the crown; a circle with a hole for the head.

Bundled
A stage in the sequence of mass production where all the cut pieces are bunched together and **docketed** ready to go on to the next stage of production.

Burberry
A waterproof coat using a patent water repellent.

Bustier
A boned bodice.

Button cards
A card on which a wide selection of button styles is offered by button manufacturers to garment producers.

Buyers
A term that has come to mean the professionals employed by retail companies – department stores, consortia, boutiques and buying companies – to select from designers and wholesale companies the items they think will sell next season.

Buying in
A term used for the procedure where the designer/wholesaler buys extra items designed and made by an outside house to supplement a collection, perhaps to complete the items in a range.

Calico
Unbleached cotton fabric used for making prototypes or toiles, which comes in different weights.

Camera Nazionale della Moda Italiana
The non-profit-making association that governs, coordinates and promotes the development of Italian fashion. Under this umbrella is the Camera Nazionale dell'Alta Moda Italiana which oversees Italian haute couture.

Caplin
The ready-formed unblocked felt or straw hood with a brim shape from which a hat can be made.

Catwalk show
The parade of garments on live models from which either private or professional buyers can make a selection.

CFDA
The Council of Fashion Designers of America, which is a non-profit-making trade association whose membership consists of 258 of America's foremost fashion and accessory designers.

Chambre Syndicale	Properly known as the Chambre Syndicale de la Couture Parisienne, it is the body that approves, regulates and oversees the running of French couture houses. This is part of the larger organisation the Fédération Française de la Couture du Prêt-à-Porter des Couturiers et des Créateurs de Mode.
Classics	Garment types that do not go out of date – a cardigan, a hacking jacket, a pleated skirt – usually characterised by simple lines.
Cloche	Bell-shaped felt hood from which a brimless hat can be made (see **hood** and **caplin**).
Cloth-lay	In mass production, where many layers of cloth are laid up at once on a cutting table ready to be cut out.
Collar jig	A template for guiding the machine round the sewing edge of a collar.
Collection	A set of models or prototypes that display a designer's latest styles for the season and from which either the private buyer, in the case of couture, or the professional buyer, in the case of ready-to-wear or mass production, can select.
Collections	The plural of the above but also the name given to joint showings, for example at London Fashion Week where all the London ready-to-wear houses show together.
Colour prediction	Usually part of a fashion forecasting system where an organisation suggests the colours for the coming seasons.
Colourways	The set of alternative colours in which either a print or a garment is offered.
Como	Fabric fair specialising in silks held twice a year in the Villa d'Este at Como in Italy.
Concession shop	Usually a shop within a shop or department store which is run or licensed by a company that is not the owner of the store.
(La) confection	The French term for the wholesale dress trade.
Construction	The putting together of a garment – cut and make.
Court dressmaker	The old term for a high quality dressmaker who is not in the class of the haute couturier but aspires to this.
Couture	The highest form of dressmaking or ladies' tailoring more properly known as haute couture. See Chapter 1 for a full explanation.
Couturier	The designer/owner of a couture house.
Créateurs	The name given to that group of ready-to-wear designers who in the late 1960s and early 1970s took over the mantle of fashion leaders from the then dated couturiers.

Crown	That part of the hat that fits over the top of the head.
Cut	(1) To cut out the fabric either with scissors or with a mechanical device such as a band knife. (2) A garment's shaping or form. (3) The style or silhouette of a garment.
Cutter	This term usually applies to the person that drafts the patterns and interprets the designer's drawing in three dimensions.
Cutting out	The practice whereby the fabric is laid up on a table and cut to the pattern piece shapes either by hand, mechanically with a band knife or by a computer-aided cutting head.
Demob suit	At the demobilisation of the troops after World War II each British serviceman was provided with a lounge suit or demob suit.
Designer end	That part of the wholesale dress market that uses named designers and is therefore more exclusive.
Designer jeans	For the giant jeans manufacturing market many designers have either designed a range of jeans or lent their name to one.
Directrice	In couture this is the woman who runs the house under the designer.
Dirndl	A full, gathered skirt with a waistband or drawstring.
Display	In distribution this is the art of presenting merchandise to the public either in the shop window, on the counter or by static displays within the store.
Distribution	This is the means whereby the merchandise is sold to the buying public; from wholesale to retail.
Docketed	The term used in mass production for labelling the bundled, cut out pattern pieces and providing the next operative with instructions.
Drafting	The art of drawing up a pattern from measurements.
Draping	Although usually taken to mean soft, falling fabrics manipulated into folds, in workroom parlance, particularly couture, it means manipulating fabric, calico or mull, on the body or dress stand to form a pattern.
Dress industry	The term used to denote that part of the garment industry that deals with lighter clothing such as dresses, skirts, blouses and slacks as opposed to the tailoring industry.
Dress rail	The term usually applies to the rail in a shop or showroom where the garments are hung and from which the customer can select.
Dress stand	Tailor's dummy. See **body**.
Drill	A coarse, firm, hard-wearing cotton fabric. Used for overalls and summer uniforms.

Dry goods establishment Drapery store.

Duck A strong, closely woven cotton or linen fabric, especially used in tailoring for pockets.

Duffle coat A heavy-duty, knee-length, unlined overcoat with toggle fastenings.

Dummy Dress stand. See **body**.

Ethnic A look based on cultural roots – African or Indian for example.

Fabric halls Large area in a department store set aside for displaying and selling fabrics and materials.

Facing Finishing an edge by applying another layer of fabric.

Faille A heavy silk or rayon taffeta with a slightly ribbed surface.

Felt makers Manufacturers of the felted wool or felted fur fibre that is called felt for the millinery trade.

FGI The Fashion Group International, which is a global non-profit association of over 6000 professionals of achievement and influence representing all areas of the fashion, apparel, accessories, beauty and home industries with its headquarters in New York.

Finishing Method of preventing the raw edge of the fabric from fraying either by hand oversewing, hemming or mechanical oversewing.

First sample This can mean either the prototype or the first try-out by the manufacturer from the prototype. The term tends to apply to ready-to-wear or mass production.

Fit The term used to describe how well the garment fits the body.

Fitter Primarily a couture term for the head of the workroom, also known as the première (de l'atelier) who is responsible for converting the designer's sketch into a pattern and then a toile and finally a finished garment. She also has the responsibility of fitting this garment on either the client or the model and running the workroom and managing her team of dressmakers, finishers and apprentices.

Fitting The process whereby the garment is tried out on the client or model for style and fit. It usually takes several fittings to achieve the level required by both the designer and the fitter.

Flat pattern cutting Patterns can be achieved by modelling fabric on the dress stand or by drafting a pattern on the flat, from blocks or templates – the former is more usually employed in couture and the latter in ready-to-wear or mass production.

Flou A term used, particularly in couture, to describe the art of draping or making soft-falling, fluid, often bias cut garments especially dresses. The flou workroom was set aside for this practice with its own première (often herself called the flou) and staff.

Flower makers Now greatly reduced in number, these small factories and large workrooms specialised in producing high quality, usually silk, flowers for trimming hats and clothing.

Forecasts Method of foretelling fashion trends, colours and fabrics.

Free form A sculptural shape that hangs from the shoulders, apparently independent of the body. Especially associated with Balenciaga and his adherents.

Grader The specialist who practises **grading**.

Grading The method whereby different sizes can be cut from one master pattern – a practice vital to both the ready-to-wear and mass production industries. Formerly using complicated mathematical formulae and requiring specialist staff, the practice is now partially computerised.

Grain lines The lines that run parallel to the edge or **selvedge** of the fabric (along the warp). These lines are of vital importance to make sure the pattern is properly and accurately laid on the fabric. Grain line indications will have been marked on the pattern pieces.

Greige A neutral-coloured cloth that can easily be piece-dyed according to the demand for a particular colour.

Grey cloth See **greige**.

Hand More usually the term used in couture for the operative seamstress or tailor.

Hat block See **blocks**.

Haute couture Literally 'high dressmaking', more usually shortened to couture.

Hem Border made by turning in the edge of a fabric or garment and sewing it down. The art of making this as invisible as possible was part of the repertoire of a good seamstress: in couture a good hem can seem like a work of art.

Hemmer The mechanical device employed in ready-to-wear and mass production to turn up hems, often called 'blind' as no stitches show on the right side of the fabric.

Hoods The basic shapes, either **caplin** or **cloche**, in felt or straw from which a hat can be shaped or moulded.

House The design establishment usually using the name of the designer – the House of Dior, the House of Cardin etc. Originating with the couture houses but later to be used by ready-to-wear companies and designers.

IMB Cologne	A fair held every three years in Cologne demonstrating the latest developments in garment technology from heavy machinery to the latest fasteners.
Incorporated Society of London Fashion Designers	The now defunct association formed to approve, regulate and oversee the London couture houses (see Appendix I).
Interlining	Layer of material between the lining and the shell or outer fabric of the garment which helps it to keep its shape.
Journeyman	A tailoring operative who has completed an apprenticeship and can be hired by the day.
Just-in-time technology	Made possible by the introduction of computer-aided manufacture, just-in-time is a system whereby the processes from design to finished garment can be achieved so quickly that nothing is produced until it is needed, thus obviating storage and waiting time.
Kimono sleeve	A sleeve cut in one with the body of the garment.
Laid up	The term used for spreading cloth on a table and placing pattern pieces out on this prior to cutting either manually or by machine.
Lay or lay plan	Method whereby the pattern pieces are laid out on the fabric in the most economical way. Today in mass production this is done by a computer-aided system.
Levels	Types or stages of quality in manufacture, for example couture, ready-to-wear and mass production.
Line	Specialised goods or particular garment range.
Machinist	The operative who assembles the garment by machine – usually a power machine on a mass production shop floor.
Mac(k)intosh	The waterproof coat that was made possible by the invention in 1823 by Charles Macintosh of a patent rubber solution used to treat fabric.
Made-to-measure	A garment made to the client's individual measurements. All couture garments are made in this way and it is the distinguishing factor in their manufacture. Menswear tailoring is known as bespoke, but is in fact also made-to-measure.
Make	The way a garment is sewn together – in mass production called **assembly**.
Mannequin de ville	These were the first 'live' models. Society beauties of the late 19th and early 20th centuries who frequented the most fashionable events were given wardrobes of clothes for the season by the great Paris couturiers to wear at the best places.
Mantuamaker	The earlier term for dressmaker used particularly in the 16th, 17th and 18th centuries. They were usually men.

Mark up	In the fashion economy this is one of the most important terms. It is where the profit on a garment is made and it means the percentage added to the cost price to make either the wholesale price or the retail price.
Marketing	The strategy whereby goods are offered to the market, i.e. the appropriate buying public.
Mass production	To produce in great quantities by a standardised, mechanised process. Ready-to-wear is a form of mass production; however, the term has come to mean the volume market.
Merchandising	This is the science of making sure that the right garments are in the right place at the right time.
Millinery	The art or craft of making hats.
Moda In	Italian fabric fair held in Milan in the spring and autumn of each year.
Model	(1) The prototype or first sample garment. (2) Girl or boy used for showing clothes.
Model girl	The girl on whom the model, first sample or prototype has been fitted and tried out and who wears it, usually at a showing or fashion show where private clients or professional buyers can select the items they require for next season. In the past, couture houses hired a set of girls for the season and held showings every day for a month or more; nowadays this would be far too expensive. Some of these model girls became photographic models and started to earn huge salaries and later developed into the super-models we know today.
Model gown	An exclusive dress more usually from the wholesale dress industry, presumably originally under the pretence that it was the first sample and therefore the only one of its type, which of course would be untrue. Also called model.
Modelling	(1) Usually the couture practice of forming the pattern on the stand or body using calico or mull. (2) The art of showing the clothes to the designer, the buyers or the public on the model girl or male model.
Mood board	A design presentation technique usually used in mass production, showing suggested designs, fabrics, colours and trends.
Mull	A lightweight muslin fabric that is used to drape or create shapes and patterns on the dress stand, especially when the final item will itself be in a lightweight fabric such as chiffon or crepe de chine.
Muslin	Another term for **mull**.
Nest	A term used in mass production for grading when all sizes are shown at once.

New Look	Created by Christian Dior in 1947, it was the turning point in post-war fashion. It introduced full, ankle-length skirts, sloping shoulders, and a feeling of turn-of-the-century opulence that many in the aftermath of World War II found quite shocking.
Ninon	Semi-transparent cotton voile.
Norfolk jacket	A shooting jacket invented by King Edward VII when Prince of Wales. Its characteristic is the four box-pleats that run through the body of the jacket to give the shooting arm extra ease of movement.
Notch	The indentation or nick in a lapel, where the top collar meets the turned back body of the garment.
Off-the-peg	Another term for ready-to-wear, meaning bought directly from the rail.
One-way fabrics	Some fabrics such as velvet can be used only in one direction, otherwise the pile will make it look a different colour. Many prints and checks have similar limitations.
Open to buy	The budget, especially that of a buyer.
Outwork factories	Manufacturers that are independent units whose time and product can be bought by design houses to manufacture their garments. The system is often called CMT or cut, make and trim.
Overlocking	The mechanised method of finishing seam allowances inside a garment to neaten them and prevent them from fraying.
Oversewing	The hand work method of finishing seam allowances inside a garment.
Pad-stitching	A type of stitching that is done in tailoring to attach the interlining to the body of the garment and to help mould it into the required shape.
Pattern	The template from which a garment will be cut.
Pattern cutter	The person who interprets the designer's sketch into a pattern, oversees the making of a toile and the first sample, supervises the fittings and makes sure the item proceeds into production.
Peak	Visor-like section on a cap that shades the eyes.
Phasing	The technique of releasing only part of a collection at a time in order to stimulate sales.
Pile	Fur-like surface on fabric formed from cut loops.
Pitti Filati	Yarn fair held twice a year in Florence in summer and winter.
Point d'esprit	Semi-transparent dotted cotton voile.
Point of sale	On or at the sales counter.
Prato Expo	Fabric fair held twice a year in Florence in spring and autumn.

Première	Also known as première de l'atelier, or in English the first fitter and head of the workroom. This is the person responsible in a couture house for the interpretation of the designer's sketch into a finished garment via toile, fittings and first model. The première also has to fit the client when the first model or sample is converted to the client's measurements.
Première Vision	Cloth trade fair held twice a year in Paris in March and October where most designers choose their cloth for the next season.
Press list	This is the database of fashion journalists, press offices and media contacts kept and updated by fashion houses, fashion organisations and major retailers.
Prêt-à-porter	(1) The French term for ready-to-wear. The off-the-peg method of selling garments which does not involve making to individual measurements (see Chapter 2). (2) The huge twice yearly trade fair of French ready-to-wear held in the Porte de Versailles, Paris. Not to be confused with the designer ready-to-wear Créateurs de Mode shows which are held in the Carrousel du Louvre.
Production line	The 'conveyer belt' system used in the wholesale garment industry where the fabric is cut, the cut pieces are passed on to machinists, the assembled garment is passed on to the finishers, then to the pressing unit, subsequently to the labeller and finally to the packers.
Production manager	The person who directs the method of work in a garment mass production factory.
Production pattern	The perfected pattern developed from the sample or designer pattern which will be used in the garment mass production process; it can be in card, plastic or within the memory of the computer-aided cutting head.
Production unit	Manufacturing outwork factory.
Prototype	The first sample try-out.
Rag trade	The garment industry.
Raglan	Loose-fitting coat with a full-cut sleeve and a seam extending at an angle from each armhole to the collar in the front and back. Named after the 1st Baron Raglan, commander of the British troops in the Crimea.
Rail	The dress rail in a shop or designer showroom on which garments are hung for selection.
Range building	This is a very important part of the designer's repertoire. A range is a small, linked group of garments that need to compliment each other from a buying point of view.
Ready-mades	The earlier term used for ready-to-wear clothing, often used in a derogatory way and comparing it with made-to-measure clothing.

Ready-to-wear (RTW)	The off-the-peg method of selling garments which does not involve making to individual measurements (see Chapter 2).
Reefer	A heavy-duty, hip-length over-jacket, usually in navy melton cloth, based on the naval jacket.
Revers	The point of a garment, normally a jacket, that is turned back as a lapel.
Roughs	The designer's preliminary drawings from which he/she can select ideas that might go forward into production.
Safari jacket	Belted, single-breasted shirt-jacket with four patch pockets and flaps.
Sample cutter	An operative who cuts single layers of cloth using shears for samples.
Sample machinist	A specialist machinist who works with the designer and the pattern cutter to produce the first sample or prototype.
Samples	Prototype or first model.
Seam	Join or stitch line between the edges of two pieces of cloth.
Seam allowance	The distance between a stitch line and the cut edge of a fabric – it is relatively wide in couture as it can be trimmed later, but in mass production and ready-to-wear it has to be much more exact as it is the guide edge for the machinist to sew against at 0.6 cm, 1 cm and 1.5 cm etc.
Season	The two seasons in fashion are spring/summer and autumn/winter.
Second fitting	A couture term where the client is given another fitting to check that those alterations made at the first fitting were appropriate. A third fitting may be called for if the item still does not seem right or small adjustments to the fit need to be made.
Seconde	The second fitter or the second in command after the première in a couture house.
Selecting	The job of choosing the items from the designer or wholesaler.
Self	In the same fabric as the body of the garment – this particularly applies to belts, covered buttons, facings and trimmings.
Selvedge	The neat, longitudinal edge of woven fabric, parallel to the warp and grain. Its purpose is to keep the outside edges of the fabric firm during subsequent processes.
Shell	The body of a garment before the collar, sleeves, hems or lining have been added.
Shooting jacket	A sports jacket of wool that often has a reinforced, suede shoulder panel. Used for sports, including shooting and hunting.
Showing	The event where the collection or this season's style are shown either to professional buyers or to the public.

Sizing	Scientific method of making garments that can fit a variety of shapes and sizes – different countries have different size formulas. The number or letter designating the dimensions of a ready-made garment is based on the measurement of the chest/bust, waist, inseam or inside leg, neck and sleeves.
Sourcing	In modern mass production terms this means looking for factories throughout the world who will take on production, and it also means taking into consideration the principles of ethical trading. A design company does not want to find it is employing child labour or using factories with bad conditions for its workers.
Sparterie	A straw-like material that is used to try out hat shapes before the design is made up in fabric, felt or straw. It is also used as a hat block when stiffened with shellac.
Spreading machine	The machine used in mass production to spread the rolls of fabric on to the cutting table before cutting out. Many layers have to be laid up at once, accurately and quickly, and the selvedge has to be parallel to the table edge.
Stitch	Single pass of the needle in hand sewing, single complete movement in machine sewing.
Stock/textile cutter	The operative who cuts out work in bulk using a **band knife** or **straight knife**.
Store	Or department store, originating from the idea that if items were bought in bulk, stored and later selected from a large range, prices would be more competitive and the choice and variety much wider.
Straight knife	Most commonly an 8 or 12 inch straight blade which cuts using an up and down movement.
Straw plait	A narrow ribbon of straw made by twisting or plaiting which can be machined together to make hats.
Strip straw	Another term for the above.
Sweat shop	A garment factory or workshop where the conditions are abominable and the operatives grossly overworked. From the Victorian term sweating – working in such close proximity and at such a pace that this unhygienic state was inevitable.
Tacking	See **basting**.
Tailleur	The old word for a woman's tailored suit, from the French for tailor.
Tailor tack	A method of marking out the pattern shape with needle and double thread on two layers at once. This is afterwards cut leaving tufts that mark the sewing line.

Tailoring industry   This is the industry that grew from the outwork tailoring factories and became the wholesale tailoring industry which still produces both men's and women's wear outer garments – coats, suits and men's tailored trousers.

Tailor's chalk   Specially hardened chalk that comes in either a flattened rectangular or triangular shape for marking out the pattern directly on to the cloth in tailoring. Can also be used to identify alterations.

Toile   A mock-up made in calico to test the pattern for style and fit before the item is cut out in the chosen fabric.

Trace tack   Like tailor tacking above, but uses a single thread on a single layer of fabric to mark out the pattern pieces.

Trade fairs   International yarn, textile and garment fairs usually held twice yearly and which have become the preferred method of buying and selling these goods to the trade. The industrial equipment fairs usually show every three years.

Trench coat   The semi-waterproof greatcoat that was supplied to the troops in World War I to wear in the trenches; now a fashion item.

Tropical uniform   Specially adapted service uniforms for the tropics in unlined, lightweight fabrics often supplied with shorts.

Vendeuse   The expert couture saleswoman with whom the client places an order for a garment from the collection and who supervises the fittings, liaises with the designer and arranges delivery.

Volume production   Term used to describe the manufacture of very large numbers of garments in mass production.

Wardrobe   The selection of items a client makes for the season; for example, two country suits, two town suits, three afternoon dresses, two cocktail dresses, three evening dresses and one ball gown.

Wholesale dress industry   The mass production garment industry that includes both ready-to-wear and mass production but not couture. A huge industry that produces all light clothing dresses, blouses, skirts, shirts, trousers, nightwear and lingerie.

Index